Urban Education

Recent Titles in
Handbooks for Educators and Parents

Urban Education

A Handbook for Educators and Parents

Donna Adair Breault and Louise Anderson Allen

HANDBOOKS FOR EDUCATORS AND PARENTS
James T. Sears, Series Editor

PRAEGER

Westport, Connecticut
London

Library of Congress Cataloging-in-Publication Data

Breault, Donna Adair.
  Urban education : a handbook for educators and parents / Donna Adair Breault
and Louise Anderson Allen.
      p.   cm.—(Handbooks for educators and parents, ISSN 1554–6039)
    Includes bibliographical references and index.
    ISBN 978–0–313–33674–4 (alk. paper)
    1. Education, Urban—United States—Handbooks, manuals, etc.   I. Allen,
Louise Anderson, 1949–   II. Title.
    LC5131.B74   2008
    370.9173′2—dc22   2008022053

British Library Cataloguing in Publication Data is available.

Copyright © 2008 by Greenwood Publishing Group, Inc.

Library of Congress Catalog Card Number: 2008022053
ISBN: 978–0–313–33674–4
ISSN: 1554–6039

First published in 2008

Praeger Publishers, 88 Post Road West, Westport, CT 06881
An imprint of Greenwood Publishing Group, Inc.
www.praeger.com

Printed in the United States of America

The paper used in this book complies with the
Permanent Paper Standard issued by the National
Information Standards Organization (Z39.48–1984).

10 9 8 7 6 5 4 3 2 1

Contents

Series Foreword

How can I advocate for my child? What are the best school practices in teaching diverse learners? What programs are most effective in enhancing learning? These simple but profoundly important questions are the heart of this book series.

This handbook is a practical guide for parents/families and a standard reference resource for educators and libraries. The entire series provides an overview of contemporary research, theories, practices, policy issues, and instructional approaches on a variety of timely and important educational topics. It also gives straightforward recommendations for evaluating curriculum and advocating for children in schools.

Written in clear language, each handbook is divided into three major sections. An overview of the topic, in the first part, provides a framework for understanding the topic in terms of research and policy and summarizes popular approaches, programs, and curricula. The next two sections go into greater depth in a manner most appropriate either for educators or parents, including an annotated bibliography of useful print, audio/video, and electronic resources within each section. Part two is written for teachers, administrators, allied professionals, and those who are studying for such professions. It gives a concise overview of current and cutting-edge research and scholarship, details on research-based effective programs and best practices, and a guide for evaluating and implementing such programs and practices. The third part is written directly for parents and families. It provides an overview of specific issues of concern to parents, implications from research for everyday family life, and strategies for supporting their (and others') children through involvement in schools and civic life.

In *Urban Education: A Handbook for Educators and Parents*, Donna Adair Breault and Louise Anderson Allen address a key area demographic for education reform. If we are truly to bring about "meaningful and sustainable change" in public education, then ground zero is the urban community. The so-called new urbanism has brought renewal to residential housing and a return of residents from the suburbs and exurbs. However, top-down reforms most notably No Child Left Behind have done little to assist in this urban renaissance. If reform is to be both meaningful and sustainable, then it has to be a local and collective effort among teachers, parents, students working within the business community, community organizations, and places of worship. In short, it requires all of us to recognize that we are stakeholders in what happens or does not happen in the education of young people living within our cities. It also means we must assume individual responsibility to learn about curriculum and pedagogy, to inquire into the allocation of resources, assignment of personnel, standards for learning, and styles of leadership, and to pose hard questions at those in position of authority as well as to our young people and ourselves. Failure only requires individual scapegoats, success mandates personal action. And, as the authors conclude, assuming such personal responsibility requires a communitarian ethic:

> It is often difficult for individuals to take the initiative to connect with those around them in public spaces, but if you embark on a community project of planning and change, you create a space where members of your community can come together and feel connected.

Democracy requires public education. Urban schools are the heart of the American experiment. As such, they must exemplify excellence in not only curriculum and pedagogy but in those values that are imbued in everyday school life and through principles of interpersonal interaction: dialogic understanding, transparency, and inclusivity. This handbook is a manual for democratic action based on solid research, effective practice, and sound theory. It is an owner's manual for those of us who wish to reclaim the new urbanism in schooling.

James T. Sears
Series Editor

PART I

Introduction

CHAPTER 1

History and Hope of
Urban Education

INTRODUCTION

This book hopes to offer an overview of the challenges facing urban schools so that parents, educators, and community members—the stakeholders of urban schools can be better informed about the impact of federal laws such as No Child Left Behind (NCLB) and how they affect the educational needs and futures of the students in urban schools. To achieve this, we first offer a survey of the history of urban education, and also explore the theories and research that address the nature of urban schools and their operations. Additionally, we will provide recommendations throughout the book to assist urban stakeholders (parents, educators, students and community members) in the development of their civic capacity to pursue common goals. Civic capacity requires accepting one's role within a community and seeing what needs to be done as a civic obligation. It represents the ability, knowledge and skills by which urban stakeholders can accept their civic responsibility in participating in the reform of the community—and this includes education.

The term "urban" has a number of meanings. Urban education refers to schools in a central city or otherwise metropolitan area. For some, the determination of the urban city designation is based upon population levels. For example, the Bureau of the U.S. Census defines urban as any area populated by 2,500 people or more while the bureau characterizes a Metropolitan Statistical Area (MSA) as a city of 50,000 or more. However, mere geography or population does not address the characteristics found within urban areas that are most relevant to urban schools. To address this, sociologist Louis Wirth defines a city as a large, dense, and permanent settlement with heterogeneous individuals. According to Wirth, this definition allows consideration for significant social characteristics. For the purposes of this book, we focus on the certain social characteristics that have been associated with urban areas and which are highly relevant when addressing urban school reform. We examine urban schools within the context of high concentrations of poverty and generally at-risk children. According to the U.S. Census Bureau, children are at risk if they have any of the following characteristics: not living with both parents, head of household is a high school dropout, the family income is below the poverty level, family members have no steady employment, family is receiving welfare, or the family has no health insurance. Since urban schools educate 40 percent of the country's low-income students and 75 percent of its minority students, we can assume with some certainty that many of our urban youth who are educated within public schools fall within the at-risk categories described above.

America's 100 largest school districts represent less than 1 percent of the districts in the nation but educate 23 percent of all public school students while employing 21 percent of the nation's teachers. Most urban educational systems are in large and growing districts that have a considerable percentage of students of color, who are also typically English as a second language (ESL) students. There are also great numbers of special education students and the schools have a higher than average teacher–student ratios and higher than average percentage of students whose families are at or near the federal poverty line. Thus, the combination of these characteristics in each district emphasizes the uniqueness of the local nature of urban education. Further within each of these districts there are a variation of size and a range of wealth.

With urban dropout rates hovering at 50 percent and test scores well below national averages, stakeholders—parents, teachers, students, and community members who serve in or are served by urban schools—need to better understand the challenges that urban education represents. There are two primary reasons why we need to do this: first, because the long-term movement of the country's population is shifting from rural to urban/suburban centers with skyrocketing enrollments in urban public schools; and second, because immigration into the country has increased dramatically with the most newly arriving immigrants settling in urban cities with ethnic communities. Thus, urbanization along with increased enrollments fueled by immigration is overwhelming urban public schools. Along with the scrambled collection of social, financial, and political issues that compound educational decisions, urban education will become increasingly important in the country's national consciousness.

There is also a moral obligation to act based upon this greater understanding when considered within the context of the recent NCLB legislation. The centerpiece of this law is to highlight and solve the problems often associated with urban schools. The goal of the act is to decrease the achievement gap among diverse groups of students, especially those who are socially and economically disenfranchised from mainstream middle-class America. By examining how this legislation has been used in many of the nation's urban school systems, this handbook identifies the challenges that face urban schools today because of this legislation.

Not surprisingly then, NCLB's accountability measures have the greatest impact on schools serving the urban poor. Many of the schools in America's large cities are not making the annual yearly progress (AYP), the necessary level of academic achievement as defined by the legislation and as measured by test scores. Urban schools with large numbers of special needs populations (ESL, learning disabled, etc.) face additional challenges of showing academic gains with these students. When urban schools do not measure up, they often receive very prescriptive curriculum packages and additional testing materials on reading and math that take the place of such subjects as art, music, and social studies. As a result, irrelevant, disconnected skill-based instruction is given to the least advantaged children in poor urban schools. Genuine, relevant, connected to real life learning becomes secondary in an attempt to raise test scores. Meanwhile, more affluent schools demonstrating higher degrees of success on the standardized tests are given greater flexibility in both their curriculum and instruction. Consequently, the heightened emphasis on test scores resulting from NCLB has generated a new form of discrimination.

The challenges created by the accountability measures under NCLB can take a toll on the professional self-esteem of teachers—particularly those in urban schools. Imagine a second grade teacher in an urban school. She has twenty-three new students in the fall. Over half of her class are students who have transferred from other schools during the year. Some of these students have been in three or more schools in the three years they have been in school. A few of the students in her class are refugees from a war-torn country, and they have never attended school. Nearly a third of her students have very limited English proficiency, and their parents do not speak English, so the only time they hear the language in order to reinforce what they are learning is when they are in school. Ninety percent of this teacher's class qualifies for the free lunch program. Of these, some often do not have food at home so the one meal they count on consistently is the free lunch. Some of the students have parents who work at nights, so they are left at home unsupervised. Violence and crime are very real to these students. Some of the students have older brothers and sisters who are involved in gangs and/or who are under the supervision of the juvenile justice system. All of them know people in their communities who are the perpetrators or victims of serious crimes.

In spite of these challenges, this teacher works hard all year. She spends hours at night planning for meaningful lessons. She comes in early and stays late to work one-on-one with many of her students. She spends her own money to help take care of some of their personal needs—a coat for one student, breakfast for others, and school supplies for many. By spring, this teacher sees students who entered her class as nonreaders now read independently and show an interest in books. She sees students master math concepts and solve problems that in the fall would bring them to tears. She sees children who come out of their shells and show excitement about what they are learning. She sees children who may have had problems with truancy in the past but who are in school every day. She also sees parents who were afraid to come to school and who did not want to talk to teachers on the phone now come in and volunteer in the classroom.

This teacher can see evidence of all her hard work all around her. Yet, when the test scores come back, the progress the students made just wasn't quite enough in one academic area or all of her students made adequate progress except for the five who qualify for special education. Since schools and teachers are judged on performance in all areas and for all special student populations, this teacher did not make AYP with her students. This judgment overshadows all of the other evidence. Suddenly the teacher believes she is a failure.

What can teachers do to prevent the decimation of their professional self-esteem? First, they need to recognize achievements and challenges beyond those characterized by the current federal legislation. Administrators, parents, and community stakeholders can help by articulating what matters most to them and by finding good ways to measure and honor those things in the classrooms and school. Second, teachers need to take time to seek out and/or create networks of support both within and outside of the school. All teachers are facing these challenges, and when they come together to address them they can help put things into perspective and seek out possible ways to cope. Third, teachers need to find safe ways to be political without jeopardizing their positions. Teachers can form book clubs at local bookstores for parents, teachers, and community members to read books that address the current issues within urban schools. These book-study groups will help to inform those not in schools each day that some of the current policies have detrimental effects within many urban schools. Teachers can also organize mass mailings to the editors of their local papers when test scores are published to show the newspaper and the community that the test scores do not accurately represent all the work going on in urban schools. Finally, teachers need to set priorities for themselves to help them recognize success—however small it may seem—within their own classrooms. "Leaving no child behind" is a tall order—one that can never be filled. Teachers need to determine for themselves what they hope to achieve in their classrooms and then recognize and celebrate when they reach their goals.

Tips for Teachers

✎ Recognize achievements and challenges beyond those characterized by the federal government.

✎ Take time to seek out and or create networks of support both inside and outside of school.

✎ Find safe ways to be political without jeopardizing your position.

✎ Set priorities in order to see small successes throughout the school year.

THE COLOR OF REFORM

When we speak of urban schools, we are speaking about children of color. Political science professor Peter Irons noted that while the general population of a city may be majority white, there was not a single school district among the nation's twenty-five largest central city school districts that has a majority of white students at the turn of this century. With more children in urban schools, this may be our nation's most important challenge, for if these schools fail, the nation fails. An additional concern is that these schools remain unequal because segregation by race correlates with segregation by poverty. The poorest students are those of color; fewer whites experience impoverished schools to the degree that African Americans or Latinos do. Further, Harvard's 2001 report, "Schools More Separate," identifies a strong relationship between a school's poverty level, the quality of instruction, and thus student achievement. Said differently, most children of color attend inner-city schools where they are more likely to have ill-prepared teachers who engage in skill and drill, worksheet instruction or what we call a pedagogy of poverty. By contrast, enriched instruction that is relevant to students' lives is left outside the classroom while students sit muted, merely repeating only what the teacher offers. Students are not actively engaged in the learning but are passive recipients of whatever knowledge is going to be on the test.

Media images of urban centers paint urban schools as overcrowded places filled with drugs and poverty with centers of violence and racial strife, and beset by political malfeasance. Thus, the urban landscape shapes the country's perception of "emergent American culture" and that in turn will shape how policy makers indirectly and educators directly will create appropriate and inappropriate instructional strategies for these children of color. The mainstream media has also portrayed urban education as corrupt, inefficient, and failing. This is not a new phenomenon. Thirty years ago, David

Tyack, a Stanford University professor, contended that urban education has offered opportunity for some while reinforcing injustice for others. He argued that schools have rarely taught the children of the poor effectively, despite their intentions. In fact, Tyack asserted that the increasing rules and regulations of urban schools have "continued positions and outworn practices" such as intelligence testing, tracking, and vocational schools that have hurt rather than helped students. Thus, it appears that even today we still have much to learn about urban education and it would be foolish to ignore what we do know about its history.

REFORM AND THE CULT OF EFFICIENCY

To understand the significance and complexity of urban education, it is important to explore the development of urban schools over time. Tyack offers a valuable history of urban education that identified the leaders of urban education from the nineteenth century onward and defined how their work has impacted public schools into the twentieth-first century. One of the most noteworthy innovations, the graded classroom, came from John Philbrick, the superintendent of the Boston Public Schools. He and other educational leaders who followed him were convinced that there was "one best way" to supervise urban schools. By implementing the right decisions and establishing patterns of leadership and management, children would thrive and progress in classrooms where a male supervisor examined female teachers' work. In fact, superintendents liked to boast that they could sit at their desk and tell by their clock what each child was studying at that hour. At this same time, massive waves of immigrant children were transforming and nearly overwhelming urban schools. As school leaders sought to organize crowded schools, they created bureaucratic rituals and practices. For example, leaders linked organization and bureaucracy to the country's quest for modernization by teaching students punctuality, regularity, attention, and silence as necessary habits for citizens of an industrial civilization. By comparing schools to businesses such as factories, railroads, or even the army, school leaders consciously tried to use the business model as a blueprint to mold and shape urban education.

First, the school leaders had to get the children to school, because school attendance had been voluntary. Eventually, most states legislatures passed compulsory attendance laws. Second, school leaders had to determine the most efficient way to classify students. In years past, students of all ages were grouped together in one-room schoolhouses. Philbrick introduced the egg crate school in Boston in 1847 with the Quincy Grammar School, which had twelve rooms where students were grouped according to their academic achievement. He also argued for male administrators to have greater control of the school with female assistants in each room. Thus, not only did

Philbrick create the graded school, he also created the gender-based conception of appropriate roles for males and females in education.

From 1890 until 1920 during the height of the Progressive Era, school leaders, including university professors, battled local school leaders for control, and increasingly took their frustrations to powerful businessmen. Forging an alliance, they would reshape urban education into a business with a corporate school board composed of successful people that could (theoretically) conduct its business within an hour's meeting weekly. This urban progressive movement revered both educated mastery and competence along with disinterested public service. The school leaders believed that if they "took the politics" out of schools by letting the professionals make the decisions, then the clients (students) would best be served. What the school leaders wanted was a hierarchical structure with objective rules that were consistent and rational. What they got were political systems where the superintendents made the decisions, along with greater authority for managers. In nearly all urban districts, many segments of the working-class community were disenfranchised from participating in local decisions.

EDUCATION FOR THE TIMES

The Great Depression altered the balance between the corporate world and the school leaders when school budgets were threatened with deep cuts in property taxes and school spending by the business community. Educators increasingly turned their backs on business leaders and by 1935 President Roosevelt channeled money directly into the poorest school districts. Consequently, by the start of World War II, professional educators became even more isolated from business leaders and played a severely limited role in educational change.

The decade following the war brought little relief for urban education and schools were attacked by government critics, business and military leaders, and by the public. Schools were facing a multitude of babies that were born after the return of the soldiers from the war; they also needed new school buildings to house the students and teachers to fill the classrooms. At the same time that the government was fixated on the perceived external threat of the Russians and communism, less attention was paid to the growing demographic and economic changes that were taking place in the American cities—changes that would ultimately impact urban education.

From the 1960s on, education was used by each succeeding president to fulfill different roles in combating poverty to regaining our preeminent position as a world-class economic leader. But it would be Ronald Reagan and then the first George Bush who would close the door on professional educators and return education to its alliance with the business community.

In the spring of 1983, Reagan's Secretary of Education Terrel Bell and a panel of business leaders issued *A Nation at Risk*. Using harsh language and military terminology to shock the American public, the panel blamed schools for producing mediocrity and pushing the country toward economic ruin. The American public clamored for reform and Reagan reversed his stand, embracing education and the professionalization of teachers. Business leaders and politically savvy governors and later presidents such as Clinton and the junior Bush have responded to this clarion call for school reform and they have increasingly controlled the discourse since 1984.

ECONOMIC UNCERTAINTY AND EDUCATIONAL ACCOUNTABILITY

Throughout the 1990s, words such as accountability, excellence, standards, and reform gained popular usage and attention. Spurred by alarm over the federal budget deficit, a changing, postindustrial economy, and the pressures of globalization, education reform became a major vehicle for political realignment in the 1980s and 1990s, culminating in in the 2002 federal legislation, NCLB. The law supposedly emphasizes local control, flexibility for local officials and parental involvement. There are, however, grave implications within this legislation for urban schools filled with children of color and newly arrived immigrants. States are required to use their assessments in measuring reading and math achievement in grades 3–8 but to use a national test on a sample of 4th and 8th graders every other year. Further, states are required to demonstrate academic proficiency for all students within twelve years. Schools that are unable to make adequate yearly progress (AYP) for two years are required to allow students to exercise public school choice and go elsewhere. It is this last provision that stands perhaps both as a death knell and/or a clarion call for urban schools and the reform of public education.

URBAN CHALLENGES TODAY

The current accountability movement spawned by the NCLB legislation has a significant challenge for educators, parents, and guardians of urban youth. The social and economic realities of our cities' youth—factors completely out of the control of the schools themselves—contribute to poor performance on standardized tests. As urban schools fail to meet their AYP, they and the children they serve are dubbed "failures." With such onerous distinctions, urban schools are faced with more and more prescriptions and test-preparation materials in the hopes of showing improvement while more affluent schools are, for the most part, left alone. When numerical indicators derived from standardized tests become the primary way we judge schooling, our urban youth suffer the most. Prescriptive curricular packages promising immediate quantifiable returns on state-mandated tests offer little in the way of meaningful learning. This further widens the gap between the students in these failing schools and the more affluent students who are protected from such desperate measures. Thus, the accountability movement creates a new form of discrimination—where poor and minority youth of urban schools are given fragmented and lifeless curriculum in the form of test preparation materials. For some, the scores do go up, but rising test scores are merely indicators that actual learning is going down.

As Alfie Kohn—a prominent educator considered by the *New York Times* to be the most outspoken critic of testing—notes, increased test scores on current standardized tests indicate that teachers have shifted their focus to the lowest levels of learning at the expense of teaching students to think critically. Kohn quotes research that has shown decreases in critical thinking as test scores increase. He also cites a number of examples from districts across the country where teachers stop good teaching to shift to drill and mindless worksheets weeks before testing. In other schools, new material is not introduced weeks before the test in order to review and practice for the test. He also shows how in a number of states, social studies, science, and other subjects are reduced if not eliminated for large portions of the year in an effort to prepare for the tests. While these practices can be seen in a variety of schools, they are particularly practiced in urban settings where there is more pressure to increase sagging test scores.

Just as the students of urban schools are most harshly hit by the NCLB legislation, teachers within those schools are most harshly hit in terms of their sense of efficacy and professionalism. For instance, at a recent lecture given by the superintendent of a large urban district where each elementary school had to choose a reform model to implement, a teacher asked the superintendent whether teachers in the district had been given the opportunity to determine whether their schools would adopt specific reform models. The superintendent replied that the "worst" schools in the district had not been given the opportunity to determine whether they would use particular reform models because "if they had known what they were doing in the first place they wouldn't have needed the models." Another teacher asked the same superintendent whether a teacher within her system would have the professional discretion to alter strategies within the models used in her district if such alterations may better serve students' needs. The superintendent replied that the question would have to be answered on a case-by-case basis because not all teachers could be trusted to make the right decisions for their students.

Thus, when schools fail to meet their AYP and have reform models imposed, teachers no longer have the ability to exercise professional judgment. They are required to follow very detailed directions for administering instruction, and much of the administrative support within a school or district is used to monitor whether they are following those very specific directions. Teachers have administrators doing three-minute walk-throughs (often urban teachers refer to these visits as "drive-bys") to ensure, for example, that the appropriate materials are posted on their boards, that they have the appropriate paperwork completed for each student, that they are pointing to the words in the teacher manual with the correct hand and moving that hand in the correct direction, that they are snapping their fingers at the exact moment required within the directions, that they are indicating which students are not answering correctly by putting their names on the board, and so on.

Further, by relying heavily on high priced test taking materials, urban districts may be fiscally compromising the quality of education in their districts as well as undermining the quality of instruction of their students. Numerous companies, some of whom actually created the tests themselves, are developing packaged curricular materials that all but guarantee that their implementation will ensure higher test scores. Many urban districts have implemented these prescriptive initiatives across all schools, and prescriptive programs widely implemented require "training" by outsiders to ensure all students are getting the same exposure to the materials. Thus, in school systems such as Chicago and Atlanta, the precious few professional development days scheduled are filled with outside consultants telling teachers how to implement their prescriptive materials.

Meanwhile, the financial gap is widening between affluent and poor schools. On average, poor districts received $868 less per pupil than affluent schools. In some states, the disparity is even greater. In Illinois, for example, high poverty districts received $2,026 less per child than the more affluent districts. When the fiscal disparities are coupled with the increased expenditures for prescriptive curricular materials and consultants, the gap between our nations' poor urban youth and more affluent students widens exponentially. Again, while the financial gap affects urban and nonurban schools, it should be of particular concern to stakeholders within urban schools. In urban areas, the gaps become more and more prominent because they are coupled with the compromised social structure of city systems.

Jonathan Kozol, a prominent author who studies economic disparities, contends that these gaps in funding create devastating results in city schools. The enactment of NCLB not only affects urban students, teachers, and the fiscal well being of districts, it also threatens the nature of community within urban areas. One of the four major components of NCLB involves expanding

Table 1.1.
2003 NCLB Transfer Data

City	Eligible for transfers	Actual transfers
NYC	275,000	8,000
Cleveland	17,000	58
Chicago	19,000	1,100

school options for children. Proponents of NCLB maintain that competition will produce better educational opportunities for disadvantaged students and it will force low-performing schools to improve. Under this law, if a school fails to meet its AYP goals, it is required to then offer students the option to transfer to another public school that did make AYP. As Kozol points out, this provision turns out to be more rhetoric than reality because in most urban systems there are not enough high-performing schools to which children in failing schools can transfer. Nationally, only 1 percent of eligible students actually transferred from a failing school to a high-scoring school (see Table 1.1).

If fully enacted, this component of the NCLB act could dismantle community schools within urban areas. Studies have shown, however, that this transfer option is not widely used. In one study where ten urban districts were examined, fewer than 3 percent of the students who were eligible to transfer requested to do so. In spite of the small percentage of transfer requests, no district in the study was able to approve all of the transfer requests. Further, many of the parents who were granted transfer requests ultimately chose to keep their children in their neighborhood schools. In essence, parents are forced to make a difficult decision. Either they must keep their children in schools that have been identified as low performing, or they must work to have their children accepted into higher performing schools (and perhaps performing only slightly higher than their own "failing" schools) which may require long commutes and a loss of connection to their own community.

Researchers have also found disturbing trends regarding the implications of the transfers. The Mesa, Arizona, schools are a good illustration of this point as the sending schools (the ones who lose students) in this district had a higher average poverty rate (66%) than the receiving schools (48%). First, schools that were eligible for receiving students had even lower poverty rates (28%), but they were not chosen by the students who were eligible for transfers. Then, the cost for transfers remains within the districts, thus urban districts already faced with so many other challenges have to divert some of their financial resources to support the transfer of students from one lower performing school to another. Finally, districts are compelled to support the transfers even if moving students from one school to another compromises federal desegregation efforts or further taxes overcrowded schools.

CALLING ALL STAKEHOLDERS: THE CLARION CALL FOR REAL REFORM

In spite of articulate and innovative visions for schooling, most substantive system-wide change has not occurred within most urban school districts. System-wide reform would require fast and sweeping change, and within the context of the bureaucracy of urban districts, this would largely occur, at best, through top-down mandates. Top-down management is in many ways opposite to democratic reform—and democracy is messy and takes time. The larger and more complex an organization is, the messier democracy gets. Thus, democratic school reform does not "fit" within the overall organizational structure of large urban school systems.

Given this structure and culture of districts, we look at how urban reform can and does happen at the local school level. When and if "space" is provided to engage urban schools in a change process and when they are given sufficient flexibility to initiate their own reform efforts, then democratic school reform can take place. Therefore, we offer the school as the focus of reform, arguing that all stakeholders—students, faculty and staff, administrators, parents, and community members—need to be involved in creating the kind of world in which they want to live. Pooling together diverse experiences, perceptions, and beliefs encourages broader conceptualizations of problems. More questions are asked and more suggestions are provided regarding problems. Further, collaborating increases the possible solutions to a problem—and those solutions generated are often better than those generated by individuals.

THE ORGANIZATION OF THIS BOOK

This book is divided into three parts. The second chapter in this first section introduces ideas that will help parents, teachers, administrators, and community members work together to make a difference in their schools. The chapter describes bureaucratic organizations, dynamics of change in school, and the pressures faced by urban school leaders trying to comply with NCLB guidelines. The chapter also introduces some initiatives where parents and other stakeholders respond to these issues.

Part II of this text (Chapters 3, 4, and 5) addresses educators, including teachers, administrators, and support staff. The third chapter, "Context and Challenges: Beginning the Conversation," uses ideas from both organizational theory and change theory to better understand the context of urban schooling. In addition to understanding the school as an organization, the chapter explores implications regarding demographics of urban schools as well as curriculum challenges that have emerged as a result of NCLB. The chapter uses the information regarding urban schools as complex organizations with diverse student populations to further explore the implications of recent policy initiatives (NCLB) and how those implications affect their work in urban schools.

The third chapter of this book also critiques curriculum materials that large urban districts have selected in order to raise test scores. The critique examines the rationale and content of the curriculum and, based upon the contextual framework provided in the first part of the chapter, questions the promises made regarding higher test scores. With the context of urban schools as complex organizations within diverse communities and with the critique of curriculum materials used in response to NCLB, this chapter provides a way for educators to discuss important issues regarding the work they are doing within their specific schools.

Chapter 4, "Educators as Architects of Reform: Continuing the Conversation," prepares educators to develop networks of support within their schools that will help them to bring about positive change. The aim of the chapter is to help educators identify necessary conditions for successful reform. Teachers, administrators, and other staff will identify the resources they have within their schools—human, organizational, and cultural—and they will determine how to best use these resources to meet goals for reform. Additionally, they will learn how to effectively assess their own needs in order to identify additional resources that will assist stakeholders in bringing about change. In summary, this chapter poses images of reform as both cultural and structural phenomena whereby relationships, perspective, and networks of support become the focus of educators' work. This shift in focus from traditional images of reform allows educators to create and sustain the networks and foundations necessary for positive and sustained change within their schools.

Chapter 5, "Transformative Action Plans: Enacting the Conversation," entertains various school scenarios based upon the information provided in the first two chapters. It illustrates how stakeholders in urban schools can bring about significant change. With these images of success in mind, the chapter then leads the educators through transformative action plans whereby they determine the best means through which they create the conditions they previously identified as necessary for success. The chapter also helps educators determine the best means for creating and sustaining successful schools as well as means through which they can assess their efforts and continue a cycle of successful reform.

Section III of this text (Chapters 6, 7, and 8) is written for parents, guardians, and community members who are interested in the success of urban schools. It specifically speaks to stakeholders who want to be involved in making their schools better, but who do not know how to initiate partnerships within those schools or even understand how a school system works. It also speaks to the stakeholders who have some degree of curiosity regarding their schools' performance but who may have never considered becoming active participants in bringing about change in those schools. Chapter 6, "Politics and Policies: Beginning the Conversation," maps out the political landscape surrounding urban schools, primarily the effects NCLB has on the urban poor. This chapter informs stakeholders about the actual costs of NCLB including the loss of meaningful learning within their children's classrooms. The chapter first explains the meaning of the test scores, the correlation between test scores and socioeconomic factors, and the implications of using standardized tests to define "achievement" for students, teachers, and schools. The chapter also plainly discusses research that documents that high test scores on standardized tests often mean that actual learning is *declining*. With this research in mind, the chapter argues that NCLB legislation has created a new form of discrimination wherein low-performing urban schools have to use prescriptive, drill-based curriculum materials while suburban, affluent schools have far more flexibility regarding the materials they may use in their classrooms.

Chapter 7, "Building Blocks for Reform Coalitions: Continuing the Conversation," explores the conditions necessary for stakeholders and educators to work together to improve schools. The chapter approaches the building of professional coalitions from the perspective of the parents and helps parents see ways to take initiatives in order to work with their schools. The chapter helps stakeholders become familiar with the structures of schools and the nature of change within organizations in order to see their potential roles in the work of reform. Based upon the possible relationships they can create within their specific school contexts, parents can explore what conditions are needed to develop sustaining relationships with educators.

Chapter 8, "Agents of Change: Enacting the Conversation," follows the same goals as the book's fifth chapter. It offers stakeholders images of successful parent–school partnerships in urban settings. With these images of success in mind, the chapter then leads the parents, guardians, and community members through transformative action plans whereby they determine the best means through which they create the conditions they previously identified as necessary for success both within the school system as well as through external agencies and organizations. The chapter also helps stakeholders determine the best means for creating and sustaining those conditions needed for successful school reform and help them to develop ways to assess their work and thus continue the cycle of reform over time.

REFERENCES

Check, J. (2002). *Politics, Language, and Culture: A Critical Look at Urban School Reform*. Westport, CT: Praeger.

Irons, P. (2002). *Jim Crow's Children: The Broken Promise of the Brown Decision*. New York: Viking Penguin.

Kohn, A. (1999). *The Schools our Children Deserve: Moving Beyond Traditional Classrooms and "Tougher Standards."* Boston, MA: Houghton Mifflin.

Kozol, J. (2005). *The Shame of the Nation: The Restoration of Apartheid Schooling in America*. New York: Crown.

Marshall, J. D., Sears, J. T., Allen, L. A., Roberts, P., and Schubert, W. H. (2007). *Turning Points in Curriculum: A Contemporary American Memoir* (2nd ed.). Upper Saddle Brook, NJ: Prentice Hall.

Orfield, G. (2001). *Schools More Separate: Consequences of a Decade of Resegregation*. Cambridge: Harvard Civil Rights Project.

Popham, W. J. (2003). *America's "Failing" Schools: How Parents and Teachers Can Cope with No Child Left Behind*. New York: Routledge.

——. Why standardized tests don't measure educational quality. *Educational Leadership*, 56(6), 8–15.

Tyack, D. (1974). *The One Best System: A History of American Urban Education*. Cambridge: Harvard University.

U.S. Bureau of the Census (1981). "Characteristics of the population below the poverty level: 1980." *Current Population Reports*, Series P-60. Report no. 133. Washington, DC.

Wirth, L. (1995/1938). Urbanism as a way of life. Reprinted in P. Kasinitz (Ed.), *Metropolis: Center and Symbol of Our Times*. New York: New York University Press.

CHAPTER 2

Making a Difference in Urban Schools

In the first chapter of this book, we offered an overview of the challenges facing urban schools as well as the historical context of urban education. In this chapter, we present tools to help stakeholders in urban schools—parents, teachers, administrators, and community members—use the rest of the book effectively. In order to make a difference in urban schools, we believe that these stakeholders must recognize the challenge of working within a bureaucracy. Further, they need to understand the challenges of school reform in general and how it affects urban settings in particular. Finally, we believe stakeholders need to know how to collaborate successfully. By understanding urban schools as organizations within complex settings and by understanding that reforming schools cannot and should not happen quickly, those interested in improving urban schools will be fortified with a deeper sense of what it means to be a stakeholder in an urban school. So armed, we hope parents, teachers, administrators, and community leaders who want to bring about positive change in urban schools will be able to join with others in effective collaboration to make a difference.

URBAN EDUCATION

When overhearing the words, "urban education," images of poor children, run-down buildings, and poor academic performance often come to mind. This image offers only a partial view of schools in urban settings. True, statistics cannot be ignored. According to the National Center for Education Statistics (NCES), urban children are more than twice as likely to live in poverty, to receive free or reduced price lunch, more likely to be exposed to health and safety risks, and less likely to have access to regular medical care. Further, students at urban schools are less likely to have two-parent families, are more likely to change schools frequently, and are less likely to have at least one parent in a two-parent family work-ing. Yet, the NCES also indicates that students in urban and urban high poverty schools are at least as likely to have a parent who has completed college and to have parents with high expectations who talk to them about school.

Therefore, stakeholders want to be mindful to avoid perpetuating images of urban schools that also necessarily equal poor schools. Individuals from various socioeconomic backgrounds should come together in order to create new opportunities for positive change in urban schools. For this to happen, stakeholders need to recognize that some "urban" schools do face these economic and social challenges while others may look very different and have very different levels of resources. With this in mind, what then, do "urban" schools have in common? Whether a school serves a housing project or an affluent condominium complex, it functions within a large system. As such, all urban schools operate within a bureaucracy. In order to make a significant difference within these schools, therefore, stakeholders need to understand how their schools operate within large school districts as highly bureaucratic organizations.

URBAN SCHOOLS AND BUREAUCRACY

Urban school systems are bureaucratic organizations in the classic sense as defined by the nineteenth-century sociologist Max Weber. Urban school sys-tems have a large number of people running them at a central level. The roles these individuals play within the systems are often technical, controlled, and part of a complex hierarchy of decision makers. Because of the multiple lay-ers of administration, central level administrators often experience difficulty communicating with one another and they often find themselves limited regarding the decisions they can make because those decisions are often contingent upon decisions made or to be made by others in the hierarchy of the organization. Because of this complexity, a large number of deci-sions regarding the nature and operation of urban schools are made in an attempt to keep things consistent or regular across the system. In spite of considerable differences between and among urban schools as we have in-dicated above, central-level decision makers in urban school systems often apply a "one-size-fits-all" mentality to critical decisions about curriculum, instruction, personnel, and other aspects of operating their schools.

Keeping such items as equipment, instructional resources, curriculum materials, and professional development consistent across the system based upon system-wide decision making also creates challenges for central office staff who feel distanced from the students those decisions actually affect. When there is a social and/or psychological distance between decision mak-ers and schools, other motivating factors may influence decisions rather than what is in the best interest of students. For example, a central office administrator who has secured some sort of position of power may make a decision based on keeping his or her position or advancing to a better position. Another administrator may make a choice based upon knowing those under him or her are likely to comply or because the decision will benefit others who may later be able to do him or her a favor. These factors that are not focused on the schools or the students are more likely to occur in a complex bureaucratic system where the decision makers are not in regular contact with the individuals who are affected the most by those decisions.

Consider the following example of bureaucratic decision making in urban districts: The school board of a district in a large mid-western city determined that newly hired teachers needed to be part of a three-year mentoring program that included support from an official mentor. With this charge in mind, the school system had to develop a long-range plan that would begin with one year of mentoring and within five years support a three-year mentoring program. The central office personnel responsible for setting up the mentoring program also had to develop means for identifying and training teachers as mentors. In addition, the school board charged the system with creating and implementing this program without allotting funds to make it happen. This school system hires hundreds of new teachers each year—some who are brand-new graduates of traditional teacher education programs, others who are entering from alternative certification programs, and still others who have various years of experience in other districts. How did the district respond? The central office personnel developing the program were forced to move quickly to put into operation something that would satisfy the board while trying to create something that would ultimately serve the intent of the board's charge. In other words, they were expected to change the tires on the bus while it was still running.

The individuals involved in the program encountered numerous obstacles. For example, because they had no funds to develop the program, they had to rely upon the support of local and state universities. This required forming committees and enduring countless planning meetings to generate goals, materials, format for delivery, and ways to assess participants. While the collaboration brought about new ideas, the process itself was compromised because the district staff had to create something to put into operation as quickly as possible. Further, while an administrator at the central office was given the responsibility of developing and implementing the mentoring program, she had no power to get principals to support the work by releasing mentors for training, distributing information to new teachers, and providing school-level support for each mentor and mentee to spend time together. When it was time to implement the mentoring training for new teachers, for example, the central office administrator could not find enough principals willing to let her use their schools as sites for the evening training. Securing five to ten schools for four nights in a semester—a task that would normally take a few phone calls—became a tremendous political battle that consumed a significant amount of the central office administrator's time and professional energy.

Ultimately this mid-western urban district did set up and operate a mentoring program for its new teachers. However, there were numerous complaints about the program itself. Because the central office staff had to develop the program quickly, they chose a "one-size-fits-all" route where all new teachers were treated the same. Whether the new hires were brand new to the teaching profession or had taught in other districts for a number of years, new teachers to the city system participated in the same training sessions, completed the same activities with their mentors, and completed the same type of portfolio in the end. Further, participants expressed a number of concerns regarding the quality of training within the program, the failure to communicate to new teachers about the program, consistent quality among mentors, and the ambiguity of how the program related to their future certification and employment within the district.

The plight described from this mid-western district is not unusual, and the key players in developing the program did not have bad intentions as they planned and implemented the mentoring program. The issues that emerged within the mentoring program were a result of the bureaucracy of the school district. The organization's size, complexity, and the political dynamics of the individuals involved were far too great to ensure positive change.

URBAN SCHOOLS AND REFORM

With the mid-western city district in mind, it is easier to see why reform may lag within schools and in school districts. As educators often lament, change is slow. Inevitably, reform initiatives often have opposition directly against them as well as indirectly against them with alternative initiatives. In addition, school reform tends to lag because it is often ambiguous. Unlike cells in Petri dishes, schools and research about school reform do not necessarily provide absolute truths or specific necessary steps for improvement. Because problems are identified differently and solutions are not specifically delineated, reformers find themselves going in different directions. Educators are yet another factor that may hinder reform efforts. While it would seem obvious that educators believe that all children can learn and that they would be the first to support initiatives to improve schooling, in fact, educators have a variety of means through which they respond to their specific contexts. Some educators are ambivalent toward reform initiatives while others are hostile toward particular efforts. Likewise, stakeholders from business have varied motivations and perspectives when it comes to school reform. Given their considerable presence in recent reform efforts (serving on a variety of boards and commissions regarding school reform), they are a critical factor that must be taken into consideration when trying to bring about change in urban schools. Therefore, when considering change in urban schools, one must acknowledge the political nature of the urban system as an organization and negotiate the tensions inherent within that system.

What can parents and other stakeholders do in light of the bureaucratic challenges found within urban school systems? First, parents can learn the names and positions of key players within the district. Who is in charge of curricular decisions? Who within the central office makes the final decisions regarding the allocation of resources? What roles do the associate superintendents play in relation to the superintendent? By knowing key players and the roles they play, parents and others can direct their attention and pressure toward the people who have the power to make changes within the system. Second, parents need to know the key decisions that are being made that affect their children. Are new materials being adopted? Is the district focusing most of its professional development funds on a particular type of training for teachers? If so, what is the quality and overall perspective of that training and how will it affect students? Does the district have financial decisions to make that could translate into new or renovated buildings? Parents can attend school board meetings and other open forums to get some of this information. They may also request additional information regarding such issues and if that information is considered open record, the district must provide it. Third, parents need to organize and pressure the key players to make the right decisions. As noted earlier, central office personnel who are distant from the schools and classrooms may make decisions based upon political motivation. Some central office personnel may make decisions to avoid conflict with others—the path of least resistance among fellow members of the bureaucracy. Parents and other stakeholders need to become sources of resistance when the decisions central office staff are making are not in the best interests of students. If decision makers at the central office are aware that concerned parents and community members are watching and willing to intervene when they disagree with directions the district is taking, they will have a strong motivating force that may change the way they do business.

How Can Parents Make a Difference?

✎ Know the key players in the district.

✎ Know the decisions key players are making and what those decisions mean for students.

✎ Organize and influence key decision makers to make the right decisions.

When urban schools do change quickly, they usually do so through top-down approaches to school reform that come in the form of *reform canons* adopted at the district level that then result in *trajectories of action* within the schools. Reform canons refer to the manner in which schools and/or districts adopt reform ideas completely and without question. Often these reforms are presented to stakeholders in somewhat simplistic terms, and the means through which educators implement them are spelled out matter-of-factly. One such reform canon is "brain-based research." A number of educational researchers have written articles regarding the merits of research on the brain with direct applications in the classroom. As a result, teachers implement "brain-based" strategies such as playing classical music, offering alternative lighting to the fluorescent lights in many classrooms, getting students to eat grapes before taking an exam, or gathering students in an assembly to engage in "bi-lateral marching" (swinging arms in motions opposite of the steps of the march) to prepare for a test. These and similar activities are often adopted without really questioning their validity, exploring specific research to ensure their effectiveness, or without serious consideration of the implications of choosing these strategies over other ways to spend time, resources, and intellectual energy.

When schools and districts adopt reform canons, they act in a particular way that excludes other possibilities. We refer to this phenomenon as a *trajectory of action*. Unfortunately, some strategies or practices within reform movements take a great deal of time, energy, and financial resources to implement. When this happens, some schools and districts discard previous reform strategies and practices in order to implement the new. "Writing across the curriculum" has been a popular reform in the past where teachers encourage students to write in academic areas other than English/language arts. Teachers may ask students to write a sentence explaining how they arrived at a mathematical answer. They may ask students to write an informative essay about a science or social studies concept. When teachers encourage students to write across the curriculum, they are able to reinforce writing skills and promote connections between content. However, if a school moves to some other reform such as "problem-based learning," where teachers ask students to focus on solving a problem, the same teachers may or may not use the strategies of writing across the curriculum along with the problem-based approaches. With the problem-based learning, students may solve problems in math, science, or social studies, but they may or may not write responses to those problems to the degree that they did when teachers were focused on writing across the curriculum. Reform canons like these force districts into an Etch-a-Sketch mentality—where educators, in search of quick fixes to their problems, move in one specific direction until "experts" turn the knobs and take them in another direction. Urban schools are more likely to fall into this Etch-a-Sketch mentality when their reform models and strategies are highly prescribed.

Since the current high-stakes testing and the climate of accountability affects urban districts the most, these schools and districts tend to adopt more of the prescribed trajectory of action reforms. Because schools in urban districts face higher rates of poverty and higher levels of mobility among their students, their administrators often feel a sense of urgency to produce substantial and quick increases in test scores, and these reform models make claims that they can create such increases. Many of these schools also suffer from high teacher turnover, so their administrators feel that teachers with limited teaching experience or teachers with emergency credentials can use the prescribed models with some level of success. As a result, a number of schools in urban districts are using reform models that, like the school bureaucracy, apply a one-size-fits-all mentality to teaching. Teachers receive direct instructions (some of the models go so far as to tell teachers to point to words in a book and scan the word with the finger moving in a particular direction) on how to teach, and many of the models do not allow teachers to deviate from those instructions in spite of needs within particular classrooms.

Imagine if we applied the same trajectory-of-action mind-set on raising children. Imagine a family with three children—each with his or her unique needs and personality. Imagine also that this family has been given a pre-scribed way of parenting that is to be applied to all three children. Regardless of the children's personalities, each is to be taught, corrected, and nurtured identically. We would hardly consider this effective parenting, and we imagine that it could even be considered inhumane. Yet, we do not challenge the same principles when they are applied within classrooms.

School reform models that perpetuate a trajectory of action mind-set are not only insensitive to the unique nature of schools and the students they serve, but they are also anti-intellectual. Teachers told what to do all day are robbed of their ability to think deeply about their work. When teachers are not thinking critically in their classrooms, they are far less likely to create conditions wherein their students will think critically. Therefore, many of the models that are being used in urban schools focus on the lowest levels of thinking and shortchange teachers and students from their ability to think beyond the basics. We believe it is time for stakeholders in urban schools to assess what kind of thinking really matters and to work toward ensuring that students in urban schools engage in that kind of learning.

What has sparked this wave of Etch-a-Sketch reform in urban schools? When urban leaders turn to prescribed reform models, they do so because of the standards movement in their own state and because of the No Child Left Behind Act and its required "annual yearly progress" (AYP). No Child Left Behind is federal legislation that was signed into law in January 2002. According to this law, every state, in order to receive federal aid, must put into place a set of academic standards along with a detailed testing plan to determine whether those standards are being met. Students who are in schools that do not meet the standards established by the state may move to other schools in the district, and schools that regularly fail to make AYP will be subject to corrective action. The act uses what it refers to as "annual yearly progress" as one of the main measures of a school's performance. This law requires that schools must demonstrate that their students are making progress each year. It also mandates that schools set equal increments of improvement in order to achieve 100 percent proficiency by the school year 2012–2013. In addition to ensuring that the entire school has reached a level of proficiency by 2012–2013, the school must also show how particular subgroups are also making progress. These subgroups include various races and ethnicities, economically disadvantaged students, students with disabilities, and students with limited English proficiency.

Given what we have addressed as common characteristics of urban schools, this particular requirement weighs heavily on a number of schools within urban areas. In schools where there are a significant number of students falling within special groups, the schools themselves may be showing progress, but if one particular subgroup within the school does not show the minimum amount of progress, then the school is labeled as failing. This distinction does not take into consideration the challenges of poverty and other social factors that affect test scores.

When test scores and "AYP" become the rallying cry of politicians and policy makers, many urban administrators feel the pressure to focus on the many facets of the classroom, some good and important, some not so good and meaningful things. Some leaders divert their energy to measures that will affect test scores in the short time frame they are given by their state and the federal government to demonstrate gains. Some even manipulate the status of students in their buildings and have teachers divert time and energy to test preparation materials instead of focusing on making classroom experiences more educative. Further, issues within the school that indirectly affect achievement—discipline, teacher's morale, etc.—are often ignored because schools feel pressure to focus only on "achievement" and its relationship to instruction. Meanwhile, teachers are directed to implement "best practices" without being given the opportunity to think for themselves. Therefore, the focus on reform as a trajectory of action puts schools, students, and the urban community at even greater risk for failure. Our Etch-a-Sketch reforms are moving in the direction of "progress" and "closing the achievement gap," but the means through which they are moving toward these ends are at best questionable. With this in mind, stakeholders in our urban communities need to look toward a new image for reform models that reject trajectories of action, when searching for models that provide opportunities to address the complexity of schooling.

With these challenges in mind, it is not our intention to offer simplistic recipes for urban stakeholders to enact in order to "fix" whatever problems they may see within their schools. Instead, we hope to help teachers, parents, guardians, and community members see their schools and their potential as well as the challenges within them in ways that make enactment of reform possible. To achieve this, we focus on three critical elements of educational reform: contexts, necessary conditions for success, and plans of action. First, it is critical to understand the context in which stakeholders are to become engaged. Therefore, we explore the nature of urban communities including the effects those communities have on the schools and the schools have on the communities, the nature of bureaucracy within urban school organizations, and the nature of the learning environment within urban classrooms. Second, with the contexts in mind, we explore the conditions necessary in order to respond to the challenges within urban contexts. By focusing on conditions rather than immediate "fix it" prescriptions, we hope to help stakeholders create a democratic space where they can work together in thoughtful and meaningful ways. Finally, we hope to create a framework for creating plans of action, which will vary according to the various communities and the specific stakeholders engaging in the reform. Therefore, the frameworks we offer provide flexibility for the unique circumstances through which schools and their stakeholders may be responding. With these three elements in mind—context, conditions, and action—we try to move readers beyond the Etch-a-Sketch school reform in order to the creation of democratic spaces of possibility for our nation's urban schools.

URBAN SCHOOLS: OPPORTUNITIES FOR COLLABORATION

Urban schools face a number of social and economic challenges and as a result, in searching for solutions, the school becomes a connecting point for services to solve these issues. While this characterization is accurate in a number of ways, we choose to view urban schools as having social and economic *opportunities* rather than *challenges*. In doing this, we emphasize the fact that not all urban schools are necessarily poor schools. While more schools in urban areas have higher concentrations of students who live in poverty, not all urban schools can be characterized this way. Furthermore, we consider the unique position of urban schools in relation to their surroundings as a tremendous opportunity, regardless of the socioeconomic status of the population each school serves.

Therefore, whether an urban school is situated around housing projects or around high-rise condominiums, we believe it should focus its efforts on collaboration between important stakeholders to maximize the use of valuable urban resources. With the large numbers of services, those sponsored by various levels of government as well as nonprofit and corporate sponsored, schools and their stakeholders can tap into a wealth of resources to benefit their students and their school community. A number of urban schools have created programs that tap into these services. Some of these initiatives include parent and family programs, programs for sexually active

teens, dropout prevention programs, substance abuse programs, and inte-
grated services that combined health, vocational, educational, and social
services into a single program.

While a number of the programs created to meet the needs of urban
schools begin at the highest levels of school district administration, schools
can and should take steps to create and sustain programs that specifically
meet their needs. Thus, individual schools, as well as clusters of schools that
share similar characteristics or geography and schools that are connected
because one feeds into the other, can all work together to secure important
resources for their programs. To achieve this, stakeholders need to master
five levels of collaboration in order to successfully implement and sustain
important initiatives:

- Collaboration between administrators: Administrators need to work together
  to create the institutional support for a program and to identify the specific
  needs of their school or schools.
- Collaboration between service providers and school personnel: Successful support is provided by individuals, not by agencies. Therefore, key stakeholders
  from schools need to have regular contact with their service providers to ensure
  that the support provided is appropriate for the students served.
- Collaboration between members of participating agencies: Communication is
  key in ensuring that any collaboration that is started will continue to run
  effectively.
- Collaboration between teachers, service providers, and parents: Teachers can
  serve as intermediaries between the service providers and the parents. As such,
  there should be a continual sharing of ideas and offering of feedback between
  all parties involved to ensure that the collaboration truly represents all stakeholders.
- Collaboration between and among parents, community members, and service
  providers: At times parents and other community members can serve as the
  impetus to bring about partnerships between schools and service providers
  either by making contact with the agencies themselves or providing the impetus
  for the school to do so.

These types of collaboration, however, require commitment from all
stakeholders in order for programs to be successful. Please note that it is
critical that the administration within a school take the first step. School
administrators should not wait around for services to appear at the schoolhouse door. Instead, they should go out of their way to find opportunities
to involve faculty, staff, students, parents, and urban service providers in
order to generate positive programs for their schools. To do this, administrators should reach out to their communities, get involved with community
groups and take on leadership roles within the community as representatives
from their schools. Further, they should learn about the activities of local

service agencies, set up meetings with key stakeholders within those agencies, and imagine possible collaborations that would benefit the school and community. Once possibilities are identified, administrators need to learn as much as possible about the way those service agencies operate. This will help school leaders work more effectively with these key players in creating programs within their schools and communities. Parents can assist administrators by providing information regarding opportunities for support and partnerships in their area and by letting school administrators know that they expect these partnerships to be formed and sustained.

When stakeholders come together to collaborate, they often do so based upon some sort of impetus. For some, it may be a response to an issue. The Education and Community Change Project is one such program that involves collaboration of stakeholders. This project operates within a number of districts in Arizona and California. Through this program, parents, educators, and community members try to challenge the focus of standardized testing as a way to shape school learning experiences. Instead, participants in the program encourage the use of community-based learning. For example, students in Tucson identified a number of vacant houses and lots near their school that attracted criminals. The students wrote speeches and drew maps for city council in order to persuade them to donate a lot for a garden. Students then persuaded local businesses to donate plants and an irrigation system. As a result, the community garden became a real and relevant part of the students' curriculum. Through this project the students learned how to write persuasive speeches, to calculate dimensions of the lot for the garden, to create maps, and to design and maintain a garden.

A school's comprehensive school-improvement plan may be another impetus for collaboration. The school reform model, the Accelerated School Project (ASP) was conceived, founded, and developed by Professor Henry M. Levin at Stanford University in 1986 to address communities with high-poverty and low academic performance by responding to the questions and challenges presented in the 1983 report, *A Nation at Risk: The Imperative for Educational Reform* (United States Department of Education, 1983). ASP brings together the school, parents, and community members to support three critical democratic goals: empowerment with responsibility, unity of purpose, and building on strengths. They identify problems within the school, and then work to find solutions for those problems. Since no single feature makes a school accelerated, each school community uses the Accelerated Schools process and philosophy to determine its own vision and collaboratively work to achieve its goals.

A leadership team is created to sustain the work of the project, and the focus is on the school curriculum of accelerated and authentic learning. Since many schools serve students in at-risk situations by remediating them, which all too often involves less challenging curricula and lowered expectations, Accelerated Schools take the opposite approach. Members of the school community work together to transform every classroom into a "powerful learning" environment, where students and teachers are encouraged to think creatively, explore their interests, and achieve at high levels. They offer enriched curricula and instructional programs (the kind traditionally reserved for gifted-and-talented children) to all students.

The Accelerated Schools model has been a vehicle for promoting change in schools across the nation for the past seventeen years. Since its inception in 1986–1987, Accelerated Schools have reached over 1,500 elementary, middle, and high schools. Schools that have implemented the Accelerated Schools Project report higher levels of academic achievement, higher levels of parent and community involvement, and fewer problems with discipline ASP has been impacted by recent federal mandates as well as financial restructuring across the country. ASP has recently been "re-branded" to AS PLUS in order to provide a more focused approach to support change in the teaching and learning arena in response to NCLB and the financial crunch faced by states.

Collaboration may take on multiple forms within a single school. Whether the impetus is from the school, parents, or the community, it is critical that all stakeholders are responsive and keep the needs and interests of the students first and foremost as they work together. Human nature is a powerful force. Stakeholders—particularly those who are used to being "in charge" and who may feel they have the "power"—need to check their egos at the schoolhouse door and roll up their sleeves, ready to work for positive change. The remainder of this book is dedicated to exploring the nature of that work.

REFERENCES

Adams, K.L. and D.E. Adams. (2003). *Urban Education: A Reference Handbook.* Santa Barbara, CA: ABC-CLIO.

Anyon, J. (1997). *Ghetto Schooling: A Political Economy of Urban Educational Reform.* New York: Teachers College Press.

Berliner, D.C. and Biddle, J.J. (1995). *The Manufactured Crisis: Myths, Fraud, and the Attack on America's Public Schools.* Reading, MA: Addison-Wesley.

Bolman, L. and Deal, T. (1991). *Reframing Organizations.* San Francisco, CA: Jossey-Bass.

Check, J. (2002). *Politics, Language, and Culture: A Critical Look at Urban School Reform.* Westport, CT: Praeger.

Corbett, D., Wilson, B, and Williams, B. (2002). *Effort, Excellence in Urban Classrooms: Expecting and Getting Success with All Students.* New York: Teachers College Press.

Cuban, L. and Usdan, M. (2003). *Powerful Reforms with Shallow Roots: Improving America's Urban Schools.* New York: Teachers College Press.

Curtis, M.J. and Curtis, V.A. (1990). The intervention assistance model. *Trainers Forum,* 10(1), 3–4.

Dewey, J. (1925). *Experience and Nature.* Chicago, IL: Open Court.

———. (1933). *How We Think*. Boston, MA: D. C. Heath and Company.

Elmore, R.F. (1997). The paradox of innovation in education: Cycles of reform and resilience in teaching. In A. Altshuler and R. Behn (Eds.), *Innovation in American Government* (pp. 246–273). Washington, DC: Brookings Institute Press.

Freire, P. (1998). *Pedagogy of Freedom: Ethics, Democracy, and Civic Courage*. New York: Roman & Littlefield Publishers.

Fullan, M. (1991). *The New Meaning of Educational Change*. New York: Teachers College Press.

Greene, J. (2003). *Improving Urban Education*. Washington, DC: Fannie Mae Foundation.

Henig, J., Hula, R., and Orr, M. (1999). *The Color of School Reform: Race, Politics, and the Challenge of Urban Education*. Ewing, NJ: Princeton University Press.

Herman, J.L. and Golan, S. (1993). The effects of standardized testing on teaching and schools. *Educational Measurement: Issues and Practice*, 12(4), 20–25, 41–42.

Hess, F.M. (1999). A political explanation of policy selection: The case of urban school reform. *Policy Studies Journal*, 27(3), 459–473.

Hopfenberg, W. and Levin, H., & associates (1993). *The Accelerated Schools Resource Guide*. San Francisco, CA: Jossey-Bass.

Kohn, A. (2000). Burnt at the high stakes. *Journal of Teacher Education*, 51(4), 315–327.

———. (1999). *The Schools Our Children Deserve: Moving Beyond Traditional Classrooms and "Tougher Standards."* Boston, MA: Houghton Mifflin.

Kozol, Jonathan. (2005). *The Shame of the Nation: The Restoration of Apartheid Schooling in America*. New York: Crown Publishers.

Lee, J.O. Standards, testing, and urban schools—implementing high standards in urban schools: Problems and solutions. *Phi Delta Kappan*, 84(6), 449–452.

Lewis, S., Ceperich, J., Jepson, J. (2002). *Critical Trends in Urban Education: Fifth Biennial Survey of America's Great City Schools*. Washington, DC: Council of the Great City Schools.

Lipman, P. (2004). *High Stakes Education: Inequality, Globalization, and Urban School Reform*. New York: Routledge Falmer.

Martin, S. (1994). The 1989 education summit as a defining moment in the politics of education. In K.M. Borman and N.P. Greenman (Eds.), *Changing American Education: Recapturing the Past or Inventing the Future?* (pp. 133–159). Albany: State University of New York.

McNeil, L. (2000). *Contradictions of School Reform: Educational Costs of Standardized Testing*. New York: Routledge.

Miron, L. and St. John, E., eds. (2003). *Reinterpreting Urban School Reform: Have Urban Schools Failed, or Has the Reform Movement Failed Urban Schools?* Albany, NY: SUNY Press.

National Commission on Excellence in Education. (1983). *A Nation at Risk: Report of the National Commission on Excellence in Education*. Washington DC.

No Child Left Behind Executive Summary. http://www.ed.gov/nclb/overview/intro/execsumm.html.

Phillips, V. and McCullough, L. (1990). Consultation-based programming: Instituting the collaborative ethic. *Exceptional Children*, 56, 291–304.

Popham, W. J. (2003). *America's "Failing" Schools: How Parents and Teachers Can Cope with No Child Left Behind*. New York: Routledge.

———. (1999). Why standardized tests don't measure educational quality. *Educational Leadership*, 56(6), 8–15.

Portz, J. (1996). Problem definitions and policy agendas: Shaping the educational agenda in Boston. *Policy Studies Journal*, 24, 371–386.

Steinberg, S. and Kincheloe, J., eds. (2004). *19 Urban Questions: Teaching in the City*. New York: Peter Lang.

Stohl, C. (1995). *Organizational Communication: Connectedness in Action*. Thousand Oaks, CA: Sage Publications.

Stone, C., Henig, J., Jones, B., and Pierannunzi, C. (2001). *Building Civic Capacity: The Politics of Reforming Urban Schools*. Lawrence, KS: University of Kansas Press.

Stone, C., ed. (1998). *Changing Urban Education*. Lawrence, KS: University Press of Kansas.

Tyack, D. (1972). The one best system: A historical analysis. In H.J. Walberg & A.T. Kopan (Eds.), *Rethinking Urban Education: A Sourcebook of Contemporary Issues* (pp. 231–246). San Francisco, CA: Jossey Bass.

———. (1974). *The One Best System: A History of American Urban Education*. Cambridge: Harvard University.

Voltz, D. (1998). Challenges and choices in urban education: The perceptions of teachers and principals. *Urban Education* 30, 211–228.

Wabnik, A. (April 29, 1996). Ochoa's kids show skills that count. *The Arizona Daily Star*, http://www.azstarnet.com/public/packages/iowatest/119-5062.htm.

Weber, M. (1947). *The Theory of Social and Economic Organizations*. Glencoe, IL: Free Press.

———. (1978). *Economy and Society*. Berkeley, CA: University of California Press.

Winter, G. (2004). Financial gap is widening for rich and poor schools. *New York Times*, October 6, 2004.

Wirth, L. (1995/1938). Urbanism as a way of life. Reprinted in P. Kasinitz (Ed.), *Metropolis: Center and Symbol of Our Times*. New York: New York University Press.

PART II

A Critical Conversation for Educators

CHAPTER 3

Contexts and Challenges: Beginning the Conversation

URBAN SCHOOLS AS COMPLEX LEARNING ORGANIZATIONS

For many years, schools have been observed as if they are machines. Traditional organizational theory looked at all organizations—schools among them—as machines where systems were closed and could be controlled. Making change within a "machine" organization often involved, or so it seemed, step-by-step actions taken in relation to a problem. The structure of the leadership was hierarchical and static, and the way things worked was linear. Educators were able to plan for what was ahead, and they could function fairly well even though they were isolated from the world. This is the way they have viewed schools, their relationships with others within schools, and the role of leadership in those schools. The machine image has served and may continue to serve a variety of purposes, including the images of a bureaucratic school system used in Chapter 2. However, when educators try to use those images to determine how to bring about change in these settings, they find that the urban schools of today have outgrown machine images of their structure and operations. It is time for a new image to influence how to serve students in our city schools.

How can you as administrators, teachers, and other staff in schools see your work and your school organizations differently? You can turn to images offered by a number of researchers in business and organizational theory—images from science that help. Instead of seeing schools and school districts as machines, you can look at them as complex systems that often exist in the midst of chaos. Yet, in the midst of that chaos, you can find patterns of promising trends and practices that will support and enhance what you do.

Why is it necessary to change the image of schools? Consider all of the changes in the world around you that affect what you do. The information technology revolution makes it impossible to "control" information or, for that matter, knowledge. Boundaries that were once set by the printing press no longer have any influence. In addition to the way people learn what is going on in the world, the very way they connect with the world has changed drastically through globalization. Schools are no longer part of isolated communities. Educators are no longer preparing students to stay within a small geographic area. They have to see the world in its complexity and connectedness, and they have to prepare students for that world.

Thus, with the complex world in which we exist, educators need to recognize the complexity of schools and school systems. By using complexity theory, they can see schools as complex adaptive systems (CAS), and explore what that means for their work. How do we do this? Think about a change within your school—something fairly minor. Who initiated the change? Who did it affect? What were the outcomes of that change? To what degree were the outcomes from the policy intended and expected or unintended and unexpected? Did that one change lead to others? We can see some actions in schools as influenced by the "butterfly effect"—where even the smallest of changes can have significant and unintended outcomes. This reinforces the notion that we are not in the midst of a machine-like space where things are controlled and predictable.

SCHOOLS AS COMPLEX ADAPTIVE SYSTEMS

What is complex adaptive systems (CAS)? According to organizational theorists, CAS involve individual participants or agents who are free to act in different and often unpredictable ways. While teachers and administrators are working toward similar goals within a school, each does his or her work in his or her own way. We cannot assume that everyone sees things in school the same way or responds in the same way to events, procedures, and general practices. Nevertheless, the actions of everyone in a school are connected to others and, as such, affect the school. So, when you see schools as CAS you recognize how all the idiosyncratic elements of people working together create infinite possibilities that are continually subject to change and yet all of the elements are interdependent and make up the larger organization.

How might this relate to schools? Consider a very simple policy in place in many middle and high schools: teachers are expected to stand outside their classrooms in between class changes to help monitor what goes on in the hallway between classes and to intercept any potential problems that they may encounter with students who are coming to their classrooms. While this is a simple procedure, it can be handled in a number of ways. Some teachers will consistently stand outside their doors. They may or may not attend to the nuanced behaviors of students in the hallways—some may notice direct and obvious conflict between students but they may not necessarily notice the tensions that precede such explicit and obvious conflict that may be present in subtle ways in body language, change in movement patterns among students, etc. Some teachers may engage in conversation with other teachers nearby rather than attend to the students in the hallway. Some teachers will greet their students as they enter the room while others focus on speaking to students or teachers in the hallway. Some will see the task as a policing activity and possibly bark out orders and potential consequences to students who are noisy or too rambunctious while others use the time and procedure to build relationships with students. Others will ignore the policy altogether—staying in their rooms to grade papers or to prepare for the lesson during the class change.

Does the divergent behavior among teachers have no effect other than the immediate state of supervision? How does the choice of one teacher to stay in the room affect other teachers? How might it affect the culture of the school? What message does it send to students when they see teachers respond so differently to the same policy? How might a student feel if his teacher is occupied with school gossip while the teacher down the hall demonstrates that she is genuinely interested in greeting her students at the beginning of class? What might a visitor think if she sees the very different responses to a school policy as she walks down the hall between classes? How would the overall behavior and safety of an area in the school be affected if more than one teacher in that area consistently did not come out into the hall between classes? How might a new teacher feel when his partner across the hall never comes out between classes? How will that influence his opinion of that teacher and perhaps of teachers in general? What if all but one or two teachers on a staff regularly come out into the hall between classes and yet the administration makes sweeping admonishments about the policy in a faculty meeting instead of dealing directly with the one or two offenders? Each of these potential scenarios influences the school—its culture, the way individuals within the school feel about themselves, about others, and about the school itself. The choices teachers make may also affect other policies or lead to the creation of additional policies. It may influence the use of resources in the school—consistent failure to comply with the policy may result in more incidences within the halls. The impression that the school is unsafe may force the school to use its resources on security measures that otherwise could have been handled by teachers following the policy. If the school administration uses its resources for security measures, it means they will not be able to use the funds for other things they need. The potential outcomes and implications of such a simple policy could be expanded indefinitely. When we consider all the policies and practices that go on in a school and consider the fact that they too have infinite ramifications, it is no wonder that individuals who study organizations refer to the work in organizations as existing at the "edge of chaos."

How can you learn how to do your work better if that work is done in an environment described as complex and possibly even chaotic? Scholars who study complex systems provide ways to better understand work in schools without undermining the complex nature of that work. One such scholar, Holland, identified four basic properties of CAS that can be applied within schools. The first element of schools as CAS is *aggregation*, which means the work of stakeholders in schools, while initiated by a number of different people serving very different functions, often emerges as one act. This work is a combination of the individual efforts. Much like the cells of the brain function as one, the work of stakeholders in schools becomes a single effort. For example, while individuals within a school may serve different functions in preparing for the cancer research walk, Relay for Life, some may sell baked goods to raise money while others gather the supplies needed for walkers and others walk, they are all working together toward the fight against cancer.

A second element of schools as CAS is *tagging*. This involves a common identity created by symbols or other ways people see themselves connected. Stakeholders in urban schools come from very diverse backgrounds and experiences, yet, as members of the school community, they form a common identity. Often this common identity is represented through symbols or rituals. For example, a school in our community has what some would consider being an embarrassing mascot—the owl. For anyone not familiar with the school, to say that the owl was the mascot is far from controversial. However, the school was not called the "Hollydale Owls." They were, unfortunately, called the "Hollydale Hooters." Whoever determined this mascot years ago did not anticipate the ramifications of association between the school and a particular chain of restaurants that gained popularity years following the mascot designation. Nevertheless, the faculty, students, and parents alike use the unfortunate mascot as a source of humor and connection. Each year on the last day of school the teachers provide a variety show for the students, and each year the R.H.A. (Retired Hooters Association) perform a dance to some popular song much to the hysteria of all attending. Thus, symbols, logos, and other shared images—whether they are taken seriously or not—can serve as a way to identify and connect a school and its stakeholders.

Third, complex systems like schools are *nonlinear*. You will not always get a sum that is equal to adding all the parts together. Consider the previous example of teachers monitoring hallway behavior between classes. Doubling the number of teachers in the hallway will not necessarily decrease the infractions by one-half. Adding twenty teachers to a hallway will not necessarily affect the behavior in that hallway if those twenty teachers do not make deliberate efforts to create some sort of climate and level of expectation in that hallway. Similarly, if one teacher in a hallway of twenty began to use that time to greet students in a loud and animated way and in so doing created a very positive result in student behavior, that one person has had more of an impact than the remaining nineteen. No one can predict what each element of a system will do to the entire system. In complex systems small changes may have a very large impact and large changes may, in fact, change very little in the school.

The fourth basic property of complex systems that applies to schools involves *flow*—how the efforts of a group over time will affect the school. For example, think about the potential to really impact the school environment if all the teachers in the school regularly stood outside their classrooms between each class and used that time to build sincere relationships with their students. By virtue of the teachers' presence in the hall between every class and the deliberate effort of all teachers to use that time to connect with students could drastically affect the culture of the school, and as a result, it could significantly affect how everyone feels about being there.

Four Elements of Schools as Complex Adaptive Systems

- Aggregation
- Tagging
- Nonlinearity
- Flow

What lessons can educators take from looking at schools as CAS? If schools are that complex, can you do anything that will really make a difference? Yes. You can use the four elements of schools as CAS outlined above to explore what it means to bring about change in complex urban schools.

First, you need to recognize that what each person does in a school matters. If what educators do in a school is an *aggregation* of everyone's efforts, then you cannot assume that individual acts have no effect on the school culture and climate. For example, the teacher who stays in her classroom to grade papers instead of standing out in the hall between classes affects more than herself, her classroom, and even the area in the hall that she is expected to monitor. By ignoring the school-wide expectation, that teacher affects the climate of the school—the general social atmosphere in the school, and she potentially influences the school culture—the "inner reality" of the school that includes values, rituals, and shared beliefs of those in the school. With this in mind, if a school is interested in bringing about change, all stakeholders should take some time to examine what they do or do not do that may influence the overall purpose and mission of the school. The individual may ask, "Is there anything that I am or am not doing that may have an effect on others?"

Further, because schools involve an *aggregation* of the efforts of every-one, you need to involve everyone in any desired change. Every initiative introduced into a school will be influenced by all of the stakeholders in the school. The greater the degree to which individuals buy into the initiative, the more likely the effort will be successful. Far too often we bring change into a school without consulting those who it will affect or without taking time to ensure that everyone understands the motivation behind the change and has time to determine how they feel about it.

How may *tagging* or the identity of a school influence whether or not stakeholders can make positive changes? Ask anyone in business whether identity matters in organizations, and you will hear a resounding, "Abso-lutely!" Identity within an organization—including a school—contributes to the overall success of that organization. Conversely, if an organization does not have a strong identity, it will experience problems with motivation, collaboration, and priorities. Schools need to have a strong identity in or-der to discern what matters most. Otherwise, a school is likely to jump on every bandwagon that comes its way. Schools need to make wise decisions about how to spend time, energy, and resources. That said, teachers, lead-ers, and other staffs in schools need to clearly determine what they will *not* do even more than they need to determine what they will do. Education is full of initiatives, reform models, and curriculum packages to try to address issues such as student achievement. Without a clear identity, a school may attempt too many of these initiatives. It takes a self-confident organization to say "no" to some of the mandates and initiatives that are buzzing around today.

Third, stakeholders within urban schools should embrace the nonlinear-ity of their work. This requires giving up control over what happens on a smaller scale and focusing on creating positive and nurturing environments for positive change on a larger scale—creating positive spaces for possibil-ities. Giving up control does not mean that teachers, leaders, parents, and community members become lax in their expectations. It does not mean that they do not attend to necessary details in the change process. Instead, it shifts the focus of what matters to larger ideas and aims rather than focusing on trying to control a complex environment. For example, rather than focusing on increasing the sales of wrapping paper by percent this year, a school could focus on the larger aims that were the basis of the wrapping paper sale (i.e. increased support for teachers through purchase of instructional materials) and focus on the larger ideas within correspondence and the presentations during community gatherings.

Finally, stakeholders within urban schools need to recognize that their efforts leave a legacy for future community members within the school. While on the surface stakeholders may feel that their efforts will bring about minor changes. They may, in fact, alter the culture of the school itself. As such, they should always pay close attention to the unintended messages they may be sending by virtue of their efforts. For example if the focus of their energy and conversation evolve around fund raising, then they may inadvertently promote a consumption mindset among students, teachers, and parents where their focus is on competition and making money rather than bigger ideas about schooling and community.

Lessons from Seeing Schools as Complex Adaptive Systems

✎ What each person does in a school matters

✎ It is important to involve everyone in change.

✎ A clear identity can help a school make wise choices about time, energy, and resources.

✎ Sometimes it is more important to focus the big picture and to recognize that not all details can be controlled.

✎ It is important to recognize the legacy or cultural imprint initiatives may leave in a school.

CHANGE IN SCHOOLS

So how do concerned stakeholders try to bring about change in such a complex system as a school or a school district? Older notions of change that involved control and changing systems or what we have previously referred to in this book as a trajectory-of-action mind-set does not fit with the image of schools as CAS. Michael Fullan, a prominent figure in leadership in education, challenges us to rethink change in schools from changing structures to changing cultures based upon relationships. According to Fullan, school leaders can bring about change in their schools if they use relationships to help create conditions for greater professional and collaborative capacity. The greater the degree to which leaders can engage stakeholders in committed professional communities of practice, the greater the degree to which those leaders can create and sustain successful change within their schools.

As Fullan notes, change in schools requires stakeholders to move away from structural changes and to focus on changing cultures through building meaningful relationships. With this in mind, principals need to reach out to parents and community while simultaneously supporting their teachers by helping them learn how to build relationships with others as well. This can happen only when stakeholders share a common purpose for their work and common assumptions about schooling itself. When educators recognize the critical need for relationships in order to bring about change, they can then look to parents and community members as authentic partners in bringing about meaningful and positive change. Further, realizing the need for collective efforts, principals and teachers will hopefully reach out more deliberately to parents and community members as key players in the change process.

THE NATURE OF URBAN COMMUNITIES

David Hargreaves, another prominent scholar in educational leadership, notes that many urban communities have social and cultural diversity that can have enormous potential for innovation. According to Hargreaves, cities tend to attract creative people whose energy and resources can be used to help bring about change. Urban areas have tremendous potential for innovation because of the diversity within their communities. Unfortunately, because of this diversity, some parents may feel reluctant to get involved at the school level. According to some research, while families of all income levels and from all ethnic and cultural groups tend to be involved with their children's education at home, it is primarily the white middle-class families that are more involved within the schools. Thus, there is a critical need to get underrepresented parents involved within schools. This phenomenon creates a vicious cycle of self-fulfilling prophesy. Parents with diverse cultural backgrounds may not feel comfortable coming to the school and getting more involved. Because teachers, leaders, and parents do not see the culturally diverse parents in the school, they assume these parents do not care. As a result, the parents, teachers, and leaders do not make efforts to make these absent parents feel more welcomed. Without efforts from those currently involved in schools, the parents with diverse cultural backgrounds continue to see the school as an uninviting place, and as such, they continue to stay away.

One way schools can address the disengagement of families who may not feel welcomed in the school is to engage in the community itself. Communities within cities often have a strong identity. This identity is often reinforced through physical markers such as street signs indicating "Midtown Community" or the like. In addition, small communities within cities often host festivals and other events that distinguish them from other parts of the city. Communities may also have community businesses—stores or restaurants that become common gathering places for individuals who live or work in the area. Rather than waiting for parents and community members to come to the school, the school can reach out and make connections with families through these shared events and spaces. In some areas, a school population may come largely from one large housing project or one or two neighborhoods of homes and apartments. The school could hold meetings in these community spaces rather than in the school to help ease potential anxieties some may have coming into the school. When an area within a city already has a strong and positive identity, the school should take advantage of that identity to make positive connections with others.

CURRENT CHALLENGES TO SCHOOL REFORM AND CHANGE

In addition to finding ways to engage all members of a community, urban schools are faced with the challenge of overcoming political images of what a reformed school, in fact, looks like. According to most politicians, schools are better when their test scores go up—and, in fact, that is the only time that they are better. Limiting judgments about the quality of life in schools to a standardized test score is narrow minded and just plain wrong. This limited view has some negative consequences in all schools, but the consequences are particularly significant in urban schools where test scores are not at an adequate level or not increasing to an acceptable degree as determined by state officials. Trying to bring about change in urban schools under these circumstances becomes even more challenging when leaders try to import or prescribe the kinds of things "good" schools elsewhere are doing in hopes to get the same results. These sweeping and prescriptive reforms attempt to change the structure and operations of a school without acknowledging the specific and complex context and culture of the school itself.

In urban schools where reform models have been implemented, researchers have noted a number of problems including low levels of teacher moral, a mismatch between the curriculum and the interests and abilities of the students, problems with school leadership, and clashes between models and the school cultures. We believe there are a number of problems with using prescriptive reform models to try to bring about change in urban schools. First, when these models perceive achievement in a narrowly defined way involving standardized test scores, and when they base all the functions and priorities of a model on the sole purpose of increasing test scores, they ignore far more significant and complex elements of schooling and what might constitute success. Second, when these models are implemented according to images of schools as machines, then trajectories of action deny the complexity of the stakeholders both individually and collectively who are forced into the prescriptive ways of being. Third, when schools focus on whole-school reform models they often perpetuate a false notion that schools alone can fix whatever problems seem to warrant the model in the first place. Coupled with No Child Left Behind (NCLB) rhetoric that focuses solely on the schools as the solution to our nation's current social problems, reform models do not look to concerns within the community as part of the problem nor do they seek collaborative relationships with family and community stakeholders in order to bring about positive change.

Why Using Prescriptive Reform Models Is Problematic

✎ They ignore significant and complex elements of schooling.

✎ They force stakeholders into prescriptive ways of being.

✎ They promote the notion that all social ills can be solved simply in schools.

Rather than looking to change in schools as direct movement from one practice to another, we suggest that stakeholders focus on what Peter Senge called "levers of change" in his book, *The Fifth Discipline*. According to Senge, levers are actions that bring about change because they alter behaviors of an organization as well as the individuals within the organization. Consistent with Fullan's challenges to see change in terms of relationships, seeing our work in terms of creating and sustaining levers of change forces us to refocus what we do and attend to the conditions in which we come together as a community rather than trying to do something to get direct results. As we have described previously in this book, rather than just changing actions, stakeholders interested in bringing about change should change the conditions in which people work together. It is through changing conditions that stakeholders create spaces for opportunities within their schools, and this allows for complexity and serendipity among stakeholders and within the culture of the school.

How do you see your collective work in terms of levers of change? According to Keith, you need to rethink the roles of all stakeholders. Parents serve a broader purpose than merely advocating for their own children. Community members serve a purpose beyond merely increasing their personal potential for success in the community. All stakeholders are considered agents in the creation and support of the levers of change, and all stakeholders are considered valuable resources in bringing about change within schools. While all stakeholders are valuable resources, their potential for influencing the school depends upon the degree to which school leaders within the school and/or school district work to develop their capacity for collaboration and meaningful work together.

COLLABORATION FOR CHANGE IN SCHOOLS: INVOLVING ALL STAKEHOLDERS IN THE SOLUTION: A SCENARIO TO CONSIDER

Central City Elementary School was just awarded a state grant for $10,000 to improve physical fitness for its 800 students. As a precondition for receiving the grant, the school must include school leaders, teachers, parents, and community members in the decision-making process for using the grant money. While the school has involved a wide range of stakeholders in limited ways in the past, they choose to establish an ad hoc committee to determine the best way to use the grant money for the school. At a Parent, Teacher, and Student Association (P.T.S.A.) meeting, the principal invited individuals to volunteer for this committee. In addition, the principal sent out notices to nearby businesses that have been involved with the school in the past to get community members involved as well. In the end, the ad hoc committee consisted of the assistant principal, a classroom teacher, the physical education teacher, two parents, and a local business owner.

At their first meeting, the assistant principal discussed the nature of the grant and asked the participants to talk about why they were interested in the project. This gave each member an opportunity to see the issue from the eyes of others. It also helped the parents and community members better understand what happens within the school on a daily basis. As participants introduced themselves and discussed their interest in the grant, the assistant principal listened carefully for themes regarding physical fitness and the values of the group. She then shared what she "heard" from the group introductions and asked the members of the group to respond to these themes. She also asked the group if they felt values or priorities have been neglected when thinking about physical fitness and the school. For the next half of the meeting, the assistant principal had the group brainstorm the kind of information they would need in order to set priorities and make decisions regarding the use of the grant money. Once the group determined the information they would need, the assistant principal guided the group to map out how they could get that information before the next meeting.

At the second meeting, the assistant principal asked the group to review what they had determined mattered most about physical education and the school. Based upon the review, the group identified four program priorities:

1. Physical education should be seen in terms of a healthy lifestyle and the school should not silo physical fitness into a single class or series of activities;
2. The grant should encourage a healthy lifestyle of all community members, not just the students;
3. The grant money should create and support initiatives that could be sustained after the money is gone;
4. The grant should have a measurable impact on the health and well-being of the students and community members.

With these priorities in mind, the group shared the information they had collected based upon the needs identified in the first meeting. They noted the following areas of concern based upon the information they collected:

Concerns about physical activity at school:

1. The physical fitness equipment used in the physical education classes needed updating and repair.
2. The school had experienced security issues with their playground area on one side of the school, so they no longer allowed students to go to that playground. This severely limited access to outside activity at the school with only one playground available for the 800 students.
3. The school did not have equipment that focused on different stages of physical development.
4. Scheduling conflicts and lack of personnel support limited the amount of physical education classes students could take weekly.

Concerns about health and nutrition in the school:

1. Lack of personnel support in the school cafeteria resulted in more processed and less healthy choices for lunches.
2. Soft drink and candy machines were in operation during the lunch hour in the cafeteria, and teachers, parents, and students could access them during that time. The machines did not offer healthy alternatives.
3. Students were allowed to bring snacks to school without any school-wide restrictions on the nutritional value of the snacks.

The group then discussed the information in relation to the four priorities they had just established to find areas of critical need within the school.

Between the second and third meeting the ad hoc committee held an open forum for teachers, parents, and community members to review their progress and to ensure they were responding to the general needs and priorities of the school community. They shared and explained their priorities with the group and asked for feedback. In addition, they shared the information they had gathered about the school and facilitated discussions regarding the information and the priorities established.

During the third meeting, the group discussed the feedback from the open forum and then organized what they knew about the needs of the school and the priorities of the stakeholders. The assistant principal provided a guide to help the group with its deliberations (see Table 3.1).

The assistant principal then asked the group to discuss each concern in relation to the four priorities. She encouraged them to avoid discussing what they felt was most important at this time and only work through the issues and the degree to which those issues were consistent with the priorities established earlier.

In a series of subsequent meetings, the group had to wrestle with priorities. They first determined the feasibility of what they could achieve with $10,000 and realized that money would not provide additional personnel and could

Table 3.1.
Priorities Chart

Concern	Support healthy lifestyle	Involve entire community	Sustainable after grant money is gone?	Create measurable impact
Update and repair equipment				
Improve security of second playground				
Support developmentally appropriate equipment				
Increase opportunities for physical fitness during the day				
Increase healthy choices for lunch				
Remove unhealthy choices in machines at lunch				
Expect healthy snacks while at school				

have, at best, a limited impact on the operations of the school cafeteria. They also noted that none of their suggestions really addressed the second priority: to involve the entire community. They determined that they would need to explore ways to get the community involved in addition to addressing the needs they identified within the school. Because the group based its deliberations on the framework, they were able to debate issues according to the values rather than attack the source of suggestions. In this way the disagreements did not become personal.

Once the group had worked through how it felt about the issues and possible directions they could take with the grant money, they then had to negotiate and determine how to best spend the $10,000 provided by the grant. They identified the initiatives that would not cost money first: replacing unhealthy snacks in the machines with healthy alternatives, establishing school-wide guidelines for snacks, and providing instructional materials to make the guidelines a meaningful health lesson rather than just a list of do's and don'ts. In addition, the committee proposed to make January a healthy lifestyle month and plan events that would involve parents and the community. The group then had to determine the best use of the $10,000 provided through the grant.

Ultimately, the ad hoc committee chose to update and enlarge the playground area in the secure part of the school property—including specific areas designated for use during physical education as well as spaces that were developmentally appropriate for different age groups in the school. They also invested in professional development training for teachers on how to use playground time to increase physical fitness among students through games and organized activities. They believed this use of the money was the most sustainable way to encourage healthy lifestyles among the students because it provided an infrastructure in terms of equipment and instruction to increase the level of physical activity for years to come.

The committee, however, could not stop there. They had to determine what structures needed to be in place and what individuals within the school community would need to be involved with all of the initiatives they generated. They proposed additional ad-hoc committees and timelines to achieve goals and presented these to the faculty as well.

As you can see with Central City Elementary school's efforts, the skill set for collaboration among school stakeholders included three primary capacities: communication, negotiation, and advocacy/action. Individuals working to bring about change in a school or a school system must first be able to communicate with one another. This skill includes listening to one another in an empathetic manner as well as conveying one's beliefs and feelings in ways that will help build and sustain mutual relationships rather than creating tensions or conflict that will divert efforts away from the larger purpose(s) of the collaboration. Empathy does not emerge without deliberate efforts to make it happen. Finding ways to share about one another—one's feelings, values, interests, and priorities—may help those involved better see and understand the position of others in the group. In addition, it helps to create a shared *value space*. To the degree that stakeholders can communicate what matters most to them, the group can find common ground where they see that they share the same values.

For example, in the case of Central City Elementary, the ad hoc committee needed to first understand how each person involved in the collaboration felt about physical fitness and what their primary concerns were for the children of the school. In addition, the committee needed to understand the perspectives of others—parents, teachers, and community members. Did the parents and community members understand increasing physical education time in the regular day would take away additional instructional time from the classroom teachers? Did the classroom teacher and parents and community members realize the challenges of increasing physical education when there are only two physical education teachers for the school? How would the administrator feel if teachers and parents complained about the quality of food served in the cafeteria? Do parents realize adding additional physical activity as an extracurricular opportunity will require support from the school? If the members of the ad hoc committee did not work through these potential challenges, then they would have a difficult time empathizing with one another. Further, if these ideas are not shared, then the efforts to spend the grant money may create situations in which participants question the motives of those making suggestions (i.e., what is this person getting out of a possible purchase of expensive playground equipment?).

To further support effective communication, stakeholders should establish clear rules for discussing concerns and begin with low-risk topics until sufficient trust is developed among those involved. It is also good to plan for and create a small and safe conflict to wrestle with where the stakes are low before tackling the larger and more emotionally charged aspects of the change effort. At Central City Elementary, the assistant principal achieved this in the first meeting by asking participants to describe their interests in the grant and by identifying themes the group could then discuss. In addition, the group discussed information about the school and the school's needs before they began to discuss possible ways to spend the money. In the process of discussing concerns about physical fitness in general as well as larger goals for the grant and needs of the school, the committee was able to identify clear guidelines for deliberating when it came time to determine the best use of the grant money. Creating those guidelines helped the group be productive early in the collaboration. In addition, by assessing the school first, the stakeholders not only got valuable information regarding the needs of the school, but they also practiced collaborating on issues not directly tied to the money to be spent. In addition, as they interpreted the data regarding the current conditions within the school, the group, in all likelihood, experienced small pockets of tension where not everyone saw the data the same way. This allowed the group to engage in conflict and conflict resolution before they were at a point of trying to make key decisions regarding the grant.

Developing Communication Skills

✎ Create ways to develop empathy among stakeholders.

✎ Establish clear rules for communicating.

✎ Begin with low-risk topics to allow participants to develop trusting relationships.

✎ Plan for a low-impact conflict to practice dealing with issues before. stakes are high.

Communication skills require continuous diligence in order for stakeholders to work effectively in schools. Teachers, leaders, and parents are never "done" with learning how to communicate effectively. For example, the committee at Central City Elementary focused on communication throughout their meetings and extended that communication to involve the whole school community in their open forum. Once the basic level of communication has been achieved, partners for school change need to also work on negotiation skills. Stakeholders come to the table with very different images of what is "the right thing" to do for the school or schools. Therefore, negotiation and compromise are a significant part of the collaboration. Whatever role you may play in the collaboration, you may feel that life would be much easier if everyone saw things the way you do, and it is often easy for someone with authority to exert his or her authority within a collaborative group with this in mind. However, asserting one's own views at the expense of others, while certainly more efficient, is never a good idea. Without the school community buying into the decisions, a leader has set himself or herself up for a long battle to try to implement change.

NEGOTIATING AMONG STAKEHOLDERS

Negotiation usually requires four steps: preparing for negotiation, sharing information, bargaining with one another, and then making a commitment to a decision. When preparing to negotiate, stakeholders should gather as much information about a situation as possible. Often conflicts emerge when some people involved in deliberations have more or perhaps different information than others. To the degree that collaborators can gather and share the same information, it will help level the playing field for all those involved in the negotiations. It will also prevent individuals from using their information advantage to push forward their own agenda (withholding information to prevent others from generating alternative choices for action). At Central City Elementary, the members of the ad hoc committee determined what information they needed and then divided up the work to bring that information back to the group at a subsequent meeting.

After gathering and equally sharing information, collaborators need to have mechanisms or guidelines to help them analyze the information in relation to the issues at hand. Often this basis for decision making will come from shared values and guidelines for the problem or project. At Central City Elementary, for example, the assistant principal created the table that guided the group as they discussed the seven issues they had identified in relation to the four goals they had set. Because they had a literal framework to guide their discussions, they realized they had neglected one of their goals for improved physical fitness—involving the community—with their initial proposed areas of concern.

Once information is shared with all stakeholders, then the actual bargaining or decision making can begin. It is critical to have bigger ideas or values shape the decision-making process. Otherwise disagreements can be directed at people rather than toward priorities or values of the group. Keep in mind that negotiations rarely involve distinguishing good ideas from bad ones. Instead, negotiations typically involve choosing among a series of good ideas because of limited resources. Thus, having clearly articulated priorities about the work as well as reasonable rules for communication will help to ensure that decisions are a reflection of responding to needs and values and will help to bring about positive change. For example, the ad hoc committee at Central City Elementary was able to reference their four goals throughout their deliberations, and this helped them prioritize when they realized they would not have enough resources to do everything they would like to do.

The final step among collaborators involves making decisions and committing self and resources to the decisions made. In other words, it is not enough to debate and state opinions. Stakeholders collaborating in schools need to be able to turn their ideas into action. If the ad hoc committee at Central City Elementary School had deliberated, determined what the school should do with the money, and disbanded, then there is no guarantee that their efforts would necessarily be carried out. Instead, the committee established a timeline and identified the key individuals who would need to be involved in each of the initiatives: planning and designing the new playground, setting up professional development support for teachers, changing the snack and drink options in the machines in the cafeteria, generating school guidelines for school snacks, and planning the Healthy Lifestyle Month activities for the following year. Obviously, from this very simple example we can see that collaboration is very involved and complex, and it takes a great deal of commitment among stakeholders who are willing to see it through.

Four Stages of Negotiation

✎ Preparing for negotiation

✎ Sharing information

✎ Bargaining with one another

✎ Making a commitment to a decision

CONCLUSIONS

As evident in this chapter, schools are complex places, and the ways we have looked at change in schools in the past cannot handle this complexity. Therefore, we need to shift our views of schools from machines that can be controlled to complex systems where the interaction of stakeholders can create infinite possibilities. In spite of the complexity within schools, stakeholders can still work within them to bring about change when they recognize and utilize the four properties of schools as complex systems. First, while the work of stakeholders within urban schools involves a number of different people doing a number of different things, their efforts often emerge as one act. Second, while stakeholders within urban schools come with very diverse backgrounds, experiences, and perspectives, they have a common identity by virtue of being part of the school community. Third, it is impossible to predict or control the impact of the collective efforts of a school community. While a committee seeking reform may achieve a general goal from their work, the impact of their efforts will influence much more than the initial desired results. Finally, the collective efforts of stakeholder within an urban school will influence the school exponentially over time.

When you consider schools as complex system rather than controllable machines, you realize you must move beyond traditional trajectory-of-action mind-sets in order to bring about change. With this realization in mind, you can focus on building meaningful relationships through effective collaboration, negotiation, and action. Hopefully, the guidelines outlined previously in this chapter will help you to do just that.

REFERENCES

Fullan, Michael. (2001). *The New Meaning of Educational Change*. New York: Teachers College Press.

Hargreaves, David. (2003). *Leadership for Transformation within the London Challenge*. Annual Lecture at the London Leadership Centre, May 19.

Keith, N. Z. (1996). Can urban school reform and community development be joined? The potential of community schools. *Education and Urban Society*, 28(2), 237–259.

Schaffer, E., Bedinger, S., and Gasne, B. (1997). *Special Strategies Studies Final Report*. Washington, DC: U.S. Department of Education.

Senge, P. (1990). *The Fifth Discipline: The Art and Practice of the Learning Organization*. London: Century.

Stringfield, S. (1998). An anatomy of ineffectiveness. In L. Stoll and K. Myers (Eds.), *No Quick Fixes*. London: Falmer Press, 209–221.

Stringfield, S., Winfield, L., Milsap, M., Puma, M., Gamse, B., & Randall, B. (1994). Urban and suburban/rural special strategies for educating disadvantaged children (First year report). Cambridge, MA: Abt Associates; Baltimore, MD: Johns Hopkins University (ED 369 854).

University School of Education, Cambridge, MA. Harvard Family Research Project. Available at http://www.hfrp.org/.

CHAPTER 4

Educators as Architects of Reform: Continuing the Conversation

As stakeholders in an urban school, you want to work to bring about positive change for your students and for your school community. After reading the previous chapters, you realize that you cannot just initiate a series of things to do in order to make this happen. Your school is dynamic and complex, and so you have to rethink your work toward change. Rather than thinking about change in the trajectory-of-action or Etch-a-Sketch way of doing things, you need to think about your work in terms of creating space for positive change.

We have discussed generally in the first chapters why the trajectory-of-action mind-set is difficult when thinking about school reform today. In addition to the more general or ideological concerns which we will address throughout the book, there are also some very real and practical reasons why operating under a trajectory-of-action or Etch-a-Sketch mind-set is challenging within your school—why just following a list of things to do at the exclusion of things you have known and done in the past can limit your potential. We would like to address four of these very real and practical concerns here.

First, when you think of reform in our schools in terms of trajectories of actions, in terms of what we must do in order to bring about change, most if not all of your conversations (and thus our professional identities) focus on the same subject—you. *You* need to implement this new program. You need to schedule professional development to show teachers how to implement the program. You need to monitor teachers to make sure they are implementing the program with integrity. You need to assess the students to see if they have learned what we hoped through this program. You need to implement another program because we don't like the results of the program we just implemented. What do you neglect when so much of your professional conversations focus on you? It is far too easy to lose sight of the larger purposes of school—not to mention the students themselves—when so much of what stakeholders talk about has to do with themselves. Even though they are doing these things for their students, and to some degree way back when they considered program A versus program B, they probably based that decision on something related to our school's mission, nevertheless, in the hustle and bustle of so many school reforms, these critical elements of who they are and what they should be are lost in the fray. With this in mind, we cannot emphasize this point enough: reforms will not work when they are all about "you," and when we attempt reforms as trajectories of action, they are, inevitably, about "you."

Second, when faculty and administration are so focused on what they need to do, they may fall into a pattern of judging others for what they are not doing. When we get busy and frustrated it is often tempting to begin to judge others who we perceive are not doing enough in comparison. Just consider your own homelife for an example of this. We can recall instances when we have been so busy with cleaning or attending to household chores that we tend to lash out at our spouse or partner because he is not doing enough—and in doing so negate all the things that he may have done. Just as this can create tension at home, it can create tension at school. Whenever you hear a teacher or administrator lamenting what he or she has to do, you will often hear a follow-up caveat regarding what someone else is not doing. Trajectories of action are, therefore, self-perpetuating sources of tension among faculty. Being busy creates tension and frustration. Judging others for not being busy enough compounds this tension. Thus, trying to reform through trajectories of action offers a double-blow to a school's culture and to teacher morale.

Third, when you focus your professional energy on trajectories of action, you miss out on potentially beneficial opportunities for yourselves, your school, and your students. For example, one concern we hear from a number of teachers in recent years is that they are no longer able to take advantage of teachable moments because of the rigid curriculum materials they must use in their classrooms. When a teachable moment arises, they are afraid that an administrator may come in and see that they are not "teaching" the lesson they are supposed to be teaching at that moment. The same issue is very real for schools that focus so narrowly on specific programs or series of reform actions. When an administrator is going into a room to observe whether certain checklists are visible on the wall, if an objective is written on the board, if certain documentation is filed away for each student, etc., then he or she is not noticing other very critical elements of teaching and learning. Further, when schools have their heads firmly and solely stuck in testing data, then they miss countless opportunities to provide meaningful experiences for their students. Thus, schools can be so focused on looking for official signs of implementing a program with integrity that they miss obvious signs of need or opportunity right under their professional noses.

Finally, and an extension to the third point, when you focus so much of your energy in this Etch-a-Sketch way of reform, you do so at the exclusion of all other possibilities. Not only you do not see other opportunities, but you also close yourselves off to the possibility of exploring alternative directions. After all, an Etch-a-Sketch can only go in one direction at a time. If a teacher knows that his or her administrator is coming in regularly to see particular artifacts regarding a reform model, then he or she will focus largely if not solely on those artifacts. Whatever else that teacher may know about good teaching he or she often, by necessity, has to take a back seat. Consider this following example. When one school system in an urban suburb initiated a high-stakes assessment program approximately ten years ago, teachers were forced into a whirlwind of preparation for their students. This test took place over four days, and if children did not pass it, they would not be promoted— ever. Teachers were warned that they would be subject to potential lawsuits from parents if the children failed—holding teachers literally accountable for not teaching the knowledge and skills needed for the assessments. With this in mind teachers not only scrambled to find ways to teach for the test, but they were also frantic to document everything they were teaching should they need it in court some day. During this time one of the authors was an administrator in one of these schools. In talking with the teachers, the author spoke with a group of fifth grade teachers about encouraging their students to write a paragraph to explain how they were using data in a table to solve word problems. One of the teachers responded, "Oh yeah, writing across the curriculum. We used to do that." Frantic to prepare for this high-stakes exam, this teacher and others had shifted into one way of teaching and left all other things that they knew were good practices behind. Thus, when educators operate from an Etch-a-Sketch mentality—as these teachers did and so many others do today—they do so at the exclusion of all the other promising practices they have used in the past. They are unable to find coherence in their work and in their professional lives under these conditions.

We have identified four real and practical problems for schools when they pursue reform in a trajectory of action or Etch-a-Sketch mind-set. First, schools focus on themselves instead of on their mission and their students. Second, when teachers and administrators are so consumed with what they are doing, they tend to be more judgmental of others for what they think they are not doing. Third, focusing on what schools have to do within a reform program prevents them from seeing other opportunities for themselves, their students, and their schools. Finally, focusing so singularly on a specific trajectory of action is often accomplished at the expense of all other possible ways of creating and sustaining good schools. So, what is the alternative? We argue that rather than thinking about what they need to do, schools should focus instead on the kinds of spaces they can create, occupy, and sustain. Further, we offer five reasons why we feel schools will have greater potential for success when they shift their focus from trajectories of action to seeing their work as creating and sustaining purposeful spaces.

First, when educators shift their focus from what they have to do to the kinds of spaces they need to create and sustain, they realize how much of their world is out of their control. Particularly with so much of the rhetoric of current national policies, schools are often seen as the source and remedy of most of our social problems. True, schools whose students face serious challenges at home—financial uncertainty, dysfunctional families, violent neighborhoods, etc.—cannot use those challenges as an excuse to not teach. Nevertheless, there are very real challenges that are beyond the control of the school. Further, while educators can plan curriculum and programs within the school, they cannot completely control how they will be received. Shifting emphasis from a controlling list of things to do for implementing a program to thinking about the kinds of spaces educators want to create puts this serendipity factor on the radar and helps them to respond accordingly. Again, it does not excuse teachers and leaders from doing their best. It does, however, help them focus on more important elements of their work other than seeking to control that which cannot be controlled.

Second, when educators focus their work on creating and sustaining spaces, they open themselves up to endless possibilities for their schools, communities, and students. When architects design a building or when city planners design a city space, they have a good idea of what they are creating, but they have no way of knowing all that will take place over time in that space. They are creating spaces that are open for numerous possibilities. This is an exciting way to consider school reform. We may very well know generally what we hope to achieve with our reforms—what we want to see happen in the classroom, the school, and the community. Yet, given the serendipity factor, we cannot anticipate all that will happen by virtue of that reform. For example, a teacher may offer her students a lesson about conservation and instead of just having them read an article on conservation and answering questions, she creates a more open environment with discussion and conservation projects. Her initial goal may have been for students to learn more about recycling and why it is important. In addition, her lesson may spark additional thoughts and feelings among some of her students. A student may decide that, in addition to recycling basics in his home like paper and cans, he would like to start a recycling campaign in his apartment complex—providing recycling bins in public areas in the complex. Another student may become more interested in various aspects of science that deal with global warming and its effects on the environment. Another student may start rethinking the kinds of products her family purchases that have excessive packaging and encourage her parents to reduce the amount of waste by purchasing fewer items packaged with excessive wrappers, bottles, etc. While the teacher did not indicate all these potential outcomes in his or her lesson plans, they were possibilities based upon the sort of curricular space the teacher created in the classroom. These possibilities do not merely end shortly after the lesson. The teacher has no idea how these initial ideas may influence how some of the students respond to ecological issues well into their adult life. If the teacher had taught the lesson in a way that simply sought a series of right answers to questions about conservation, she may not have achieved the same generative responses. Instead of just teaching a series of facts, the teacher created a curricular space where the students helped shape a number of possible outcomes. Similarly, when schools move away from the very prescriptive ways of reform, they can also create spaces where a number of responses—both immediate and long-term—are possible.

Third, focusing efforts on creating and sustaining spaces helps educators to distinguish between aims and outcomes—a critical element in reform efforts. Consider the act of shooting an arrow in an attempt to hit a target. The target itself is not the aim. Actually being able to aim, pull back the bow, and release it in such a way to hit the target—the achieved ability to shoot the arrow and hit the target—is actually the aim. Far too often, we confuse the two, particularly in our work in schools. To help distinguish between outcomes and aims, think about all the tedious tasks you face at home: cooking, laundry, cleaning, running errands, etc. Each task in and of itself may seem to be relatively meaningless and mundane. However, when you consider that all of those tasks combined result in you creating a particular kind of home environment for yourself and possibly a family, then those tasks take on more meaning. In and of themselves, the tasks of cooking, cleaning, and running errands are mere outcomes; your aim, on the other hand, is to create a warm and loving homelife for yourself and your family.

Similarly, when teachers attend training sessions, when principals complete necessary paperwork, and when parents offer feedback in parent forums and meetings, they are doing more than the simple acts of meeting, writing, and listening. They are helping to create the kind of space they want the school to become. This perspective helps us remember what really matters and how what we accomplish is far greater than the sum of its parts.

Fourth, creating transformative spaces in schools helps educators create a legacy for their schools and communities. When we look to buildings from the past, we see what society valued in very real ways. Whether it is the coliseum in Rome, the cathedrals of Europe, or concentration camps from World War II, the structures we have created over time reveal the best and the worst about humanity. In the same manner, your efforts—the spaces you create—become part of the narrative of your schools and the community. When you engage in school reform, you do so not only to make a difference today, but you also hope that your efforts will have long-lasting effects within the school and the community.

ARCHITECTS OF TRANSFORMATIVE SPACES

So, if educators shift the way they look at their efforts from a series of things that must be done to actually creating and sustaining spaces, then they can focus on the context in which they work as well as the conditions they put in place to make that space more consistent with their aims. If you extend this image and really consider yourselves architects of transformative spaces, you can begin to visualize all that this new way of thinking entails. For example, what drives architects when they create spaces? Certainly purpose, function, and use of resources are significant factors when they design and create spaces. To that end, we shall explore the same three criteria when discussing the spaces we create within schools and communities.

The Power of Purpose

The architect begins with purpose and considers the purpose of the space to be created in the midst of endless possibilities. He or she then makes deliberate choices based upon context, function, and resources. The architect must consider the space to be created in relation to the other spaces as well as the larger context in which the space will exist. For example, what are the implications of building an eighteen-story skyscraper next to a row of small Victorian homes? Further, the architect must consider both function and resources. Mahogany paneling, large and comfortable leather furniture, and massive ornate columns may convey a feeling of warmth and tradition that a company may want to communicate as people enter their offices. Nevertheless, that design of a space may not be the best use of an atrium where hundreds of people will move in and out as they come and go from work each day. In addition, while a family may love the look of marble and feel that it symbolizes the strength of their family bonds, it may not be financially feasible for them to build their home out of marble. Therefore, while challenges such as context, function, and resources ultimately influence the work of an architect, those challenges do not drive the design process. They are realities in the background. The architect still begins with purpose and encounters endless possibilities at the starting point for designing a space. Similarly, when educators are working in schools, they must begin with purpose and anticipate the endless possible directions they can take with that purpose in mind. The challenges they will inevitably encounter will influence the way they ultimately design the space, but they should not be the primary basis for the spaces they create.

A strong sense of purpose within a school and its community, particularly an urban school community working toward change, is absolutely vital within any organization. Purpose brings the school community together. It provides a means through which stakeholders can do meaningful work that would otherwise seem disjointed and insignificant. Purpose provides a meaningful context within which individuals see their work and their "place" within the school community. Further, a significant and well-articulated purpose can inspire and motivate stakeholders and bring them together to create meaningful change.

The Challenge of Context: Negotiating Purpose and Practice within a Bureaucracy

Have you ever had the opportunity to help a new school develop its beliefs, mission, and vision? Perhaps you may have worked with a school that revised its mission and vision? If you have ever been in a position to be a part of this experience, then perhaps you can recall the power of possibility symbolized at the beginning of the meeting with stakeholders sitting in front of large blank chart paper and countless markers. "The sky's the limit!" you may have thought as you sat there. Whatever the group can dream of—the power of imagination—can drive the process to generate an innovative mission and vision. Yes and no. There is a small footnote that we need to keep in mind: the sky is the limit as long as our beliefs, mission, and vision fit neatly into the images of schooling espoused by the school district.

An example may help elaborate upon this point. When one of the authors first took an administrative position in a large suburban district, she had to attend a series of orientation sessions. At one such session, the superintendent shared his vision for the district: world-class standards and measured student achievement. Following his brief speech about these two critical elements of his vision, the superintendent asked each new administrator to come forward, introduce himself or herself, and state his or her vision for his or her school. The new administrators came up, dutifully introduced themselves, and not surprisingly, stated that their visions for their schools were identical to the superintendent's vision. At best, the experience was an exercise in how quickly individuals could figure out how to say the exact same thing the superintendent said without using the exact same phrase. "I want all our students to exceed our system's standards so they can compete globally"; "I want our student to surpass all students around the world in their academic knowledge and skills"; "I want our students to achieve world class standards and be the best in the world." For the hundred or more new administrators, their visions for their schools were predictably identical to the superintendent's. And then this author got up and introduced herself. "I want my students to esteem something greater than themselves." The effect in the room was much like you see in the credit card commercials on television—everything stopped. All stared at the superintendent, and his look of disapproval was noted by all—including this author.

So, purpose is critical in schools, and a dynamic vision for a school can help stakeholders create and sustain transformative spaces for students. Yet, the purpose cannot contradict or appear to undermine the stated purposes and vision of the district itself. Typically a school's vision will not be at risk of actually contradicting the vision of a district—after all you will not find a district that argues that it wants its students to succeed and a school that argues that it wants its students to fail. Instead, a school may be at risk of antagonizing the district if its vision and mission focus on values that, while consistent, are not the same priorities as the school district. This is particularly challenging now when so much of the rhetoric about purpose focuses on measured achievement. A school that challenges the focus on test scores and focuses instead on democratic principles, critical capacities, or other values, may be challenged by leaders at the district level.

FIRST LINE OF RESOURCES: THE URBAN TEACHER

While the possibilities related to any given purpose are endless, stakeholders in urban schools know that their efforts to create meaningful change are limited to some degree by resources. As such, once educators have established their purpose for their school and community, they need to examine the degree to which they can create and sustain those kind of spaces based upon the resources they have. When we think about resources in a school, we often envision school supplies, facilities, and curriculum materials. However, the most important resource of any school is its teachers.

Not only are teachers the most critical resource within a school, they are also the most complex resource to sustain. As Martin Haberman, a university professor working with teachers in Milwaukee has discovered, there are many factors regarding teachers, why they may leave urban schools, and what we can do to encourage them to stay. According to Haberman, teachers in urban schools typically live in or were raised in metropolitan areas. In addition, they often attended urban schools themselves. These teachers are often members of minority groups, and many of them have experienced a period of living in poverty or know individuals who have, so they can empathize with those who are experiencing poverty. In addition, they have worked with children from diverse backgrounds, often in paid or volunteer activities. Many urban teachers have degrees in areas other than education, and they may have changed from other careers to teach in urban areas. According to Haberman, these qualities do not guarantee that teachers will stay in urban schools, but teachers exhibiting these characteristics are more likely to stay and be successful.

Teacher turnover is a significant obstacle for bringing about change in urban schools. In his research regarding teachers in urban schools, Haberman paints a bleak picture regarding teacher turnover in urban schools. He points to the nearly half a million teachers who are of a traditional age to begin teaching and who get their degrees through traditional teacher preparation institutions. Of those who are getting their teacher certification through traditional programs, less than 1.5 percent of them take positions in urban school districts. Of these, less than one in ten will stay in an urban school for more than three years.

Why do teachers leave urban schools? Studies have indicated that the most common reasons are poor working conditions and difficulty managing children. In addition, overwhelming workloads, discipline problems, lack of respect, lack of support are also contributing factors. Haberman and others have argued that some of the reasons are far more serious—an inability of teachers to work with diverse student populations that they see as "different."

Through his work with urban teachers in Milwaukee, Haberman has identified fourteen qualities that contribute to teachers staying in urban schools. First, these teachers are persistent. They continuously work to solve problems in their classrooms and work diligently to engage each of their students. They also support the integrity of the classroom experience—even if it is contradictory to current prescriptions within their schools. They navigate the requirements of reform models in order to protect the learning environment for their students. Teachers who stay are also able to translate theory into practice. Rather than merely doing what they are told is a best practice, these teachers are able to discern what is best for their students through thoughtful practice. Further, they recognize how narrow and rigid curricula have a negative effect on students and compensate for the problems children may have encountered if they had been previously exposed to such prescriptive curricula. Teachers who stay in urban schools also make personal connections with their students and take personal responsibility for the students' successes and failures. They recognize the potential drain that can be caused when working within a bureaucracy and learn to survive within it. Finally, these teachers are willing to admit to their mistakes and correct them. As such, they model learning and respect for their students.

How can urban schools create a culture of teachers who stay? Superficial mentoring programs are not sufficient. Teacher retention has to become the responsibility of all within the community—school leaders, teachers, parents, and community members. All stakeholders within a school need to create a network of support for new teachers—not just the one assigned teacher mentor and the classroom room parent. In fact, it would be better if parents who were not directly associated with the teacher, those without children in the specific class, could work with the teacher. This support structure for new teachers could be a mammoth undertaking—particularly in schools that have high annual turnovers. Nevertheless, it is precisely these schools with high turnovers that need to invest in this sort of foundational support.

As we mentioned previously, teachers are a critical and complex resource in urban schools. It will take more than merely acquiring more financial resources to influence the percentage of teachers who will stay in urban schools. In order to create a sustainable culture where teachers will want to stay, educators have to address the challenges found in urban schools that drive a number of teachers away. If educators can address these obstacles, then they can create a nurturing environment that will attract and keep highly qualified teachers.

CRISIS OF FUNCTION: OBSTACLES TO CHANGE WITHIN THE SCHOOL

Grand visions dreamt by architects will serve no real purpose if they do not "work." The spaces they create must allow those who use the space to function effectively. Likewise, educators may have articulate visions for schools and gather untold resources. Yet, if they cannot create functional spaces, they will not bring about meaningful change. In order to create functional spaces, they must first identify significant obstacles to change and then strive to overcome those obstacles.

A number of researchers have written about the challenges to school reform in urban areas. In one study of reform efforts in Chicago Public Schools, Payne and Kaba (2007) identified five significant categories of impediments to reform: social infrastructure, building level politics, instructional capacity, environmental turbulence, and the structure of support for implementation. According to the study, urban schools often operate within a culture of mistrust. Many of the issues with trust stem from cliques that form among teachers as well as from unacknowledged racial tensions. This distrust hinders communication among stakeholders and thus prevents them from learning from their mistakes. The lack of trust increases the degree to which building level politics create problems within the schools. As a result, those with power tend to do whatever necessary to preserve it, and many in leadership positions are not willing to hear criticism. In many instances, the issues that need to be addressed are not brought up because of the political and social tensions within the building.

The lack of trust also affects instructional capacity within a number of urban schools. Teachers are isolated and do not receive meaningful feedback about their teaching from their supervisors. What little professional support teachers do get often comes in the form of sporadic professional development sessions, which have been universally recognized as ineffective. These issues are compounded by the fact that the teaching force within any given urban school is fairly unstable—with as many as 30–50 percent leaving the school annually. When a staff turns over at that pace, it is difficult if not impossible to try to establish a more trusting environment.

Urban schools not only have to wrestle within the challenges within their own building, they must also deal with the challenges imposed by their district central administration. With superintendents changing in urban districts every three years on average and with key personnel in central office positions shifting frequently, working relationships between the district and the schools are in a constant state of disruption. Further, central office administrators tend to implement reform initiatives at an alarming rate. In one study of fifty-seven districts, the average urban district implemented twelve major reform initiatives in a three-year period (averaging one major reform initiative every three months). Most districts reviewed could not support schools in these new initiatives—let alone whatever initiatives the schools had adopted themselves.

Within a number of urban schools, it is not uncommon to see three or four reform initiatives at any given time—in spite of the fact that many of them have no record of successfully implementing reforms in the past. Many of these schools are operating in crisis mode and find very little time to reflect even at a basic level regarding what is happening in their schools. When schools do adopt initiatives, they often cannot follow through because they do not have the time or the resources to do so. For example, schools in Chicago had difficulty implementing a district-wide policy on school uniforms even though most of the stakeholders supported it and its implementation did not require additional resources or any sort of shift in beliefs within the schools. Nevertheless, the schools struggled with following through with the policy.

Payne and Kaba's Obstacles to Urban School Reform

- ✎ Social infrastructure
- ✎ Building-level politics
- ✎ Instructional capacity
- ✎ Environmental turbulence
- ✎ Structure of support for implementation

Why Do Some Schools Succeed?

In spite of challenges, there are successful urban schools. What do they do to overcome these obstacles? According to Cawelti (1999), these schools stay focused on their purpose, which involves helping all students succeed. Further, these schools have strong relationships with their communities. In addition, the leaders in these schools not only provide strong personal leadership, they also enable others within the school to be leaders. So leadership is found not only in the front office, it is also evident within the classrooms. These successful urban schools involve all stakeholders in their efforts, so everyone takes ownership of their success.

Why Some Urban Schools Succeed

✎ They stay focused on purpose.

✎ They have strong relationships with their communities.

✎ They have strong leaders.

✎ They involve all stakeholders in their efforts.

AN IMAGE OF PURPOSE AND POSSIBILITY: MISSION HILL SCHOOL

Mission Hill School is a public pilot school in Boston, Massachusetts. The school serves about 170 students from kindergarten to eighth grade. The pilot school program in Boston was initiated in 1995 to encourage schools to seek new innovative ways to address the needs of urban children in Boston. Schools in the program are encouraged to be catalysts for change and offer images of possibilities that could be transferred to other schools in Boston. Mission Hill maintains small, multiaged classes where the students typically spend two years with their teachers. The mission of Mission Hill School focuses on five habits of mind which are supported by habits of work. Their habits of mind include the following:

- Evidence: using scientific method and other efforts to determine the truth and/or credibility of information
- Viewpoint: looking at issues and information from different perspectives
- Connections/cause and effect: seeking patterns and consequences for events and issues
- Conjecture: using imagination to explore alternative possibilities
- Relevance: exploring the degree to which issues and information matter

These five habits are mutually interdependent and make up the necessary conditions for a well-educated person. In order to support the five habits of mind, individuals must also exhibit habits of work which include meeting deadlines, being on time, sticking to a task, not getting frustrated quickly, and hearing what others say. The Mission Hill School community believes that the purpose of education is to help families raise their children to maintain and nurture these habits in order to support a democratic society. They believe this can be achieved through love and respect for one's self and for others—helping each other to develop and maintain these habits.

While Mission Hill is a pilot school and thus freed from a number of the system regulations in the larger Boston School System, they do not operate in isolation. They are part of the Boston Pilot Schools Network that provides leadership development for directors, teachers, students, and parents in order to support democratic and shared governance models. The network also provides support in terms of assessment, political advocacy, and community organizing. In addition to the Boston Pilot Schools Network, Mission Hill has also established a support system through a number of organizations outside of the school system. These organizations include the following:

- The Center for Collaborative Education: The center serves as a catalyst helping to support independent and innovative schools to improve student learning.
- The Coalition of Essential Schools: This is a national network of schools that support successful, democratic schools.
- The Farm School: This is a working farm that serves 1,500 urban students a year to teach them the importance of farming.
- Shakespeare & Co.: This organization comes to the school and works with seventh and eighth grades students to perform Shakespeare plays.
- Urban Improv: This organization is a violence prevention program for youth that uses structured theater improvisation to teach students how to make good decisions, control impulse, and clarify values in order to deal with conflict.
- Chill: This program offers snowboarding instruction and opportunities for students.
- Northeastern University, School of Education: The teacher education program sends interns to the school each year to work in classrooms.
- Tufts University, School of Education: The teacher education program also sends interns to the school each year to work in classrooms.

Governance and operations within the school also look very different from the typical urban school. In addition to the administrative, teaching, and support staff, the school also supports a learning specialist, a family–school liaison, an occupational therapist, a curriculum specialist, and a school nurse. In addition, the school has a number of adjunct faculty that serve specific needs at specific times. The personnel structure of the school ensures that strong relationships can be built between teachers and students as well as between teachers and parents and that sufficient supports are in place for the work of the school.

Governance or decision making within the school does not reside only with the teachers and administrators. Parents are active participants in the management and operations of the school as well. The school has a governing board that meets quarterly to review the operations of the school in relation to its mission. The board reviews the schools leadership, approves staffing and budget, and helps to develop the long-range assessment tools used to assess the school and its graduates. In addition, a separate group of parents form the parent council, and they work to share information with other parents, coordinate parent volunteer opportunities, arrange school events and fundraisers, and help provide orientation to new parents.

Curriculum and assessment also look very different at Mission Hill when compared to most urban schools. The school community develops its own curriculum based upon themes. Students study topics over a four-year rotation. Students focus on one set of topics for the first four years and then another set of topics for the second four years they attend Mission Hill. This allows students to focus on in-depth understanding of fewer topics. The school community uses student assessment as a means to get to know their students better. Therefore, their assessments include daily observations, portfolio development, journals, and conferences in addition to tests and quizzes.

Deborah Meier, the founder and first principal of Mission Hill, notes a number of factors that she feels contribute to a successful urban school. First, she notes that successful urban schools must have a strong sense of collegiality among teachers. Second, she contends that big decisions need to be made inside the school and by those who will be implementing them. Meier also argues that families need to have strong ties and positive relationships with their children's teachers in urban schools. Fourth, Meier contends that urban schools need to have a strong shared vision or image of what matters most for them. Finally, Meier argues that innovative urban schools need to be given space to operate without hostility from the school district. This is more likely to happen if there is at least one person at the central office level who trusts and supports the school and its mission.

CONCLUSION

As we have noted previously and have shown through the example of Mission Hill's story, creating and sustaining transformative spaces in schools require a strong sense of purpose and creative responses regarding context, resources, and functions. Educators must find a way to simultaneously comply with restrictions and mandates from their districts while thriving according to their independent visions and momentum. Further, they must recognize that their most valuable resources are also their most complex resources. In addition to securing the other materials and facilities that they need to make a difference, educators need to be diligent and create cultures in their schools that will draw and keep highly qualified teachers. Finally, regarding functions, educators have to make sure their spaces work. They need to be fully aware of the challenges of urban contexts, recognize the degree to which those challenges are a real part of their schools and their cultures, and then fight to overcome those obstacles and create the kind of spaces in which they want to work and live. The next chapter will provide means through which educators in urban schools can do this effectively.

REFERENCES

Cawelti, G. (1999). *Portraits of Six Benchmark Schools: Diverse Approaches to Improving Student Performance*. New York: Educational Research Service.

Haberman, M. (2005). Personnel preparation and urban schools. In F. E. Obiakor and F. D. Beachum (Eds.) *Urban Education for the 21st Century*. Springfield, IL: Charles C. Thomas Publisher, 34–58.

Meier, D. (February 2002). Just let us be: The genesis of a small public school. *Educational Leadership*, 59(5), p. 76–79.

Mission Hill School Official Web site, www.missionhillschool.org. Retrieved December 12, 2007.

Mission Hill School Official Web Site www.missionhillschool.org retrieved December 12, 2007.

Sirotnik, K. A. (1990). Society, schooling, teaching, and preparing to teach. In J. Goodlad, R. Soder, and K. A. Sirotnik (Eds.) *The Moral Dimensions of Teaching* (pp. 296–327). San Francisco, CA: Jossey-Bass.

Stager and Fullan, M. (2002). *Teacher Purpose and Educational Change: Moving Toward a Broader Agenda*. Paper presented at the annual meeting of American Educational Research Association, San Francisco, CA.

Tillman, L. (2005). Mentoring new teachers: Implications for leadership practice in an urban school. *Educational Administration Quarterly*, 41(4), 609–629.

CHAPTER 5

Transformative Action Plans: Enacting the Conversation

SHIFTING FROM INCREASING CONTROL TO INCREASING UNDERSTANDING: THE POWER OF DATA IN SCHOOLS

Given our criticisms up to this point about too much focus on test scores, it may come as a surprise to some readers that we would argue for collecting and using data to help bring about meaningful change in schools. We believe data—the *right* kind of data—is critical in the change process. We further believe that stakeholders within a school are in the best position to collect and analyze this data. However, when we talk about data, we are not talking about test scores or grades at this point. We are arguing for a very different kind of data collection that is essential within schools—the messy, qualitative kind of data that sheds light on the school climate and culture as well as the kinds of experiences students are having in the classrooms. We realize the grimaces that this suggestion may cause—"What?! I'm up to my neck in testing and analyzing test data and you are telling me I need to collect more data?! Are you crazy?!" Yet, we believe that the only way to move beyond the simplistic, trajectory-of-action reform initiatives sparked by so much of the test data is to collect real, meaningful, and yes, messy data about your school and your community.

Urban educators truly interested in reform are faced with a challenge. If they want to move beyond the simplistic Etch-a-Sketch reforms typically imposed by others, then they need to understand their context well enough to discern the kinds of spaces they need to create. When schools have a strong and articulate sense of purpose and a clear understanding of the context in which they are working, then they have the prerequisite support to work toward change.

We realize that developing lines of inquiry through which to gather data beyond the data-driven culture of schools today is a substantial challenge.

However, we would argue that it is because so much of the talk about schools at the political levels involves words like "data" and "research," it is even more critical to provide the kind of data that really matters. You may find yourself thinking, "But we cannot afford to take the time and the energy to do this kind of data collection." To this we would argue, can you really afford not to? Consider how busy multinational companies are trying to compete globally and within an unstable economy. Nevertheless, in 2004, U.S. multinational companies spent over $152.4 billion in research and development. CEOs understand that they must invest in research in order to survive. It is also important to realize a very simple fact about data and schooling: what gets measured matters. Whatever becomes the subject of our inquiry becomes the focus of our work. Subsequently, what does not get measured does not matter—or at least does not matter enough. With this in mind, schools and their stakeholders need to first examine what they do and do not know about themselves and what they need to know in order to support what they have stated as their mission.

We also believe that the inquiry process through which data is gathered should include representatives of all stakeholders in the school—not just the official leaders in the school and certainly not merely some outside consultant. Inquiry into one's school and one's work can be a transformative experience, and as such, we should not hand it over to some outsider or relegate it to a handful of people in a building to do to other people. By including all stakeholders in the inquiry process, a school community will enhance the relationships of its members—which Fullan noted is a critical precondition for educational change. Further, by engaging in the inquiry as a community of stakeholders we will increase our understanding and thus our empathy of one another.

THE INQUIRY PROCESS: GETTING THE RIGHT KIND OF DATA

So how do you go about getting information about your school? What techniques and tools will help you to see your school as a complex learning organization? We believe that qualitative data is the best kind of data to collect to balance out the current focus on test scores. Qualitative data helps you to capture those things in your specific setting that are significant and meaningful, and include all the things about your school that are messy and difficult to measure. When you gather information about your school and community through qualitative means, you are able to interpret the information in relation to the important questions that stem from your larger purpose. You do not just measure something and then make a judgment about what you have measured. Instead, you see trends, patterns, and opportunities for even more questions and greater levels of understanding. As such, qualitative data are specific to your situation, and so you are collecting them to better understand your unique context—not to try to generalize to other schools.

We want to introduce five ways you can collect information about your school and community: use of artifacts, observations, focus groups, interviews, and surveys. Each of these methods can help you to capture what is unique about your school and community and what you need to explore in order to bring about change. Each of these strategies has advantages and disadvantages, so it is important to recognize why you want to use one strategy rather than another. Further, there may be questions you have that will require you to use more than one strategy to collect data in order to get the information you need.

Using Artifacts

First, artifacts are probably one of the most neglected sources of data within schools. Some schools have developed effective means for collecting artifacts about student work such as using portfolios or projects to showcase work. However, schools often fall short in utilizing the wealth of artifacts they have to show the achievements of their teachers and their school community.

Imagine that you were put in a school an hour before the school day was to begin and you were charged with judging the quality of that school. What evidence could you find that might give you some indication of the kinds of experiences students, teachers, and other stakeholders have within that school? For starters, go into the main office and see what kinds of messages visitors would get when first entering the school. Are there scrapbooks or other forms of communication that showcase the school's achievements? Does the school have letters framed from people who may have visited the school? Do they have awards displayed? Some may even have a video that runs in the front office throughout the day that tells visitors about the school. After finding evidence in the main office, you can make your way down to the media center. Look at displays and messages the media center offers. To whom are they addressed: students? parents? teachers? What kinds of messages are present within the media center? What seems to be the focus of the space—computers, books, work areas, or places where the media specialist can read to students? Does the school have a professional library for its teachers? If so, what can you observe about that area? Does it appear to be used? Does the area have any sort of messages, notices, or other evidence that the school is concerned about the professional development of its teachers? Does it appear to be accessible to parents and community members? Walk down the halls of the school. Do you see messages on the walls? If so, what is the tone and nature of those messages? Do teachers display student work out in the hall? What assumptions can you make about the curriculum of the school based upon work that is displayed?

Just walking through a school can introduce you to a number of artifacts. In addition to these, you can learn a great deal about a school by reviewing their meeting agendas for the Parent Teacher Student Association (P.T.S.A.) and for faculty meetings. You could review the Web site to see how the school presents itself to the public and what they feel is important (or not) to convey to the public. You can also review evidence from the morning shows many schools provide over closed-circuit television. Are these programs created and run by students or by the administration of a school? Even the sign-in sheet offers a wealth of information about a school. How many parents visit the school? Does it appear that they only come for lunch, or are they involved in the classrooms? If you were to analyze the sign-in sheet more carefully you might ask, "Which parents are coming in?" Is it the more affluent parents? Only those who can speak English? When one of the authors was a school administrator and trying to recruit new teachers, she would show prospective teachers the sign-in book with its long list of parent names who came in daily to help out in the classrooms. That "data" showed prospective teachers, first-hand, what kind of parent involvement he or she could expect at the school.

Here's an exercise that could help you and your school community see the value of artifacts. Challenge stakeholders to take a camera and make snapshots of artifacts over the course of a week or two. Encourage them to also find additional artifacts (memos, etc.) to bring back that will reveal something about the school. Take time at a meeting to share these artifacts. What have you learned about your school based upon all the things the stakeholders found?

Using Systematic Observations

Observations are another largely untapped resource for data in schools. Often, when teachers think about observations, they think about the evaluation system in place in their schools. In most districts, administrators are required to observe anywhere from one to three times a year. Typically, these observations are unannounced and can last anywhere from fifteen to forty-five minutes. In other schools, leaders engage in the three-minute walk-through which some of our teachers have referred to as "drive-bys." Whether administrators are observing for three minutes or thirty, these experiences often create anxiety for the teachers. They are almost always linked in some way to how the leadership of the school is evaluating the teacher and his or her performance.

We believe observations should not always be conducted only by the school administration and should not be used solely for teacher evaluation. Observations, when done deliberately and within an atmosphere of trust and support, can provide incredibly valuable information about a school, its teachers, and the curriculum. In order to make observations a positive means of gathering data, we urge schools to consider the following guidelines. First, all stakeholders should be involved when determining what to observe and how to observe it. A shared purpose in the process of making observations will help build trust and ensure consistency when observations are being conducted among a number of teachers. When stakeholders come together and determine the purpose for the observation as well as how the observations will be conducted, it helps teachers to know that the observations are not designed to generate judgments about them. Instead, they are designed to learn something about the learning environment. Thus, the observed teachers will be less likely to think about the experiences as, "Oh, they're here to observe ME." Instead, the teachers will hopefully think, "Oh, they're here to observe how students respond to higher order questioning," or whatever the purpose of the observation may be.

Second, the purpose of the observations should be directly linked to a question the school has and, as such, should limit what the observer is actually looking for in the classroom. Observations are most effective when they focus on a manageable amount of things to be observed. So much goes on in a classroom that an observer who goes in without any particular focus will not be able to record all that he or she sees and hears. Of the things the observer sees and hears, there will be even less that he or she is able to record and thus remember. In addition, schools will struggle with consistently "seeing" the same things in a series of observations because one observer may tend to focus on things that are very different from what another observer would focus on. To get a real sense of this, we encourage you to engage in a simple experiment. Gather together stakeholders who will be responsible for making observations. Show the observers a video of a teacher teaching and ask them to record what they see. Following the video, have the observers share what they recorded with one another. They (and you) may be surprised to see how very different those observations will be. When limits are set on what to be observed, it should decrease the level of variation among the observations recorded.

Third, when possible, use observation instruments to increase consistency and accuracy of observations. Scripting, or merely taking free-flowing notes while observing in a classroom, helps to get a general sense of a classroom and is an effective way to identify themes for future observations. However, when trying to address specific questions and to get consistent information from a number of classrooms to answer those questions, free-flowing notes are not nearly as effective as specific observation instruments. If an instrument is designed well, it will let the observer focus on actually observing and less on recording. Sally Zepeda has developed a number of effective observation instruments in her book, *The Instructional Leader's Guide to Informal Classroom Observations*. Whether you choose to use these instruments or not, they are good examples from which you can develop your own to suit your purposes. Developing your own instruments can provide a very clear link between the questions you have and the observations you are making to address those questions. In addition, creating your own instruments can decrease the tension or fear factor among those being observed if they played a role in creating the observation instruments that you will use.

Fourth, we believe that it is not enough to find or create effective observation instruments; you also need to train individuals to conduct the observations effectively. Observing and recording observations is not a natural process, and often people are surprised by the level of challenge they face when trying to conduct observations. Individuals who will be responsible for conducting observations within your school need to be trained on systematically and deliberately looking for things within the room, recording observations while they continue to observe.

You may very well find that while some teachers and others can use the instruments in a training scenario, they may have difficulty actually observing their peers. What if they see something that they think is a problem? What will happen if they write down something that teacher will not like? Many teachers struggle with giving any sort of negative feedback to peers. For many, their apprehensions are justified. Given the nature of teaching, many teachers take their work so personally that any statement about what is going on in their classrooms is seen as a statement about them as people. To mitigate these apprehensions, we feel it is critical to constantly point to the purpose of the observations and remind participants that they are observing classroom behaviors and phenomena—not judging the quality of teaching. To help ease tensions, it may be helpful to start with a very modest observation. Teachers can go in and observe something fairly simple and relatively unrelated to the teachers' actual teaching. For example, observers may go in and record flow of traffic or how students engage with one another. This provides practice in the classroom and may possibly reduce tensions about being observed. It may also provide a safe scenario where problems can be identified without losing critical information you hope to get with later observations.

Fifth, we encourage you to involve as many people as possible in the observation process and minimize any sense of power an individual may have over another regarding observations. Trust is always a significant factor when it comes to observations. Even very strong and confident teachers may feel apprehensive when someone comes in to observe his or her classroom. In addition, if the school has not established a trusting atmosphere, teachers may be wary of inviting other teachers into their rooms to observe. With this in mind, concerned stakeholders need to support the emotional capacity and self-esteem of teachers within the school so they will feel comfortable with others coming in to observe. Just as you cannot assume everyone will be able to use the observation instruments you choose or create, you cannot assume everyone will be "ready" for someone to come in and observe in their classrooms. In addition, using observations to gather data about your school provides an opportunity to involve more stakeholders in the change process. Encourage teachers and community members to be part of the observation team. When they help identify or create instruments and when they are trained in the observing, they will also gain a greater general understanding of what is going on in the school and develop greater empathy for teachers and administrators. Further, including parents and community members in observations sends a powerful message to these stakeholders—"We have nothing to hide."

Guidelines for Classroom Observations

✎ All stakeholders should help determine what to observe and how to observe it.

✎ Observations should be limited in focus and relate to the larger purpose of the inquiry.

✎ When possible, use observations instruments to make observations accurate and consistent.

✎ Train observers to use observation instruments effectively.

✎ Include as many stakeholders as possible in the observation process.

Using Focus Groups

A third way to gather data about your group involves focus groups. Focus groups involve getting together a group of ideally six to eight people who have something in common and having a deliberate conversation with specific questions about the inquiry at hand. Focus groups should be small enough for everyone to share but large enough that you will get diverse perspectives within the conversation. Focus groups are helpful to understand a group's perspectives, understandings, feelings, and common knowledge. They are also a good way to collect data because they play on a natural way of relating to one another—through conversation.

Why use focus groups? This data gathering method will help you build relationships among your stakeholders—a concern we will visit in greater detail in the next section of this book. So, in addition to getting important information, you will also provide opportunities for varied stakeholders to spend time together and share ideas with one another. In addition, focus groups are helpful when you want greater depth and complexity from responses. Where surveys limit responses to a scale or other narrow characterization of a question or issue, focus groups are open ended and provide opportunities for more elaborate responses. Focus groups encourage free expression, and often this free expression triggers even more detailed and thoughtful responses from others in the group. Finally, focus groups can help educate stakeholders about the issue. When you develop a survey or a protocol of questions for a one-on-one interview, participants often have to assume a particular meaning of terms, phrases, and concepts that are part of the questioning. When these same people participate in a focus group, they also get to hear others' interpretations of those words and ideas, and this gives them a larger understanding of the subject under investigation.

Do not let the informal and conversational nature of focus groups fool you. Good focus groups take a lot of planning. You will need to be very deliberate to ensure that your focus group will run smoothly and that you will get the kind of information you need from the group. In planning for a focus group, first examine the purpose of your overall inquiry and make sure using a focus group will help you achieve that purpose. Is the topic something that requires complex responses and should reflect the different perspectives, opinions, and feelings among your stakeholders? If so, then the focus group is a good option for gathering your data.

Once you have determined that a focus group is the best way to gather the information you need, you then need to make sure you have the necessary supports to run the group effectively. Who will lead the group? Do you have someone who knows how to facilitate discussions, who can encourage engagement from all, and who can prevent one or two people in the group from dominating the conversation? Can your potential facilitator encourage thoughtful answers if he or she encounters a group that initially responds superficially to the focus group questions? Can your facilitator handle potential conflicts that may arise during the process without shutting down the conversation? In addition to choosing an effective facilitator, you need to determine the best way to record what the group says. If you use a tape recorder—which we highly recommend—who will transcribe the tape in a timely manner?

With the supports in place, your next step would be to handle the logistics of a focus group. Who will you invite to participate? To what degree do they represent the school community? If you are planning on holding multiple focus group meetings, then you need to decide whether you will create focus groups that span across the various stakeholders (i.e., parents, teachers, and community members within the same focus group) or create more homogeneous groups to discuss the issues (one group for teachers, one for parents, etc.). There are advantages and disadvantages to both compositions, and the biggest factor you should consider is the current dynamics among stakeholders. Is there enough trust and understanding among the varied stakeholders that they would feel comfortable talking with one another? If so, a mixed group could be beneficial. If, on the other hand, parents may feel reluctant speaking out in front of teachers or teachers may feel uncomfortable speaking out in front of community members, then you may want to consider more homogeneous focus groups addressing the same issues.

Once you determine who you want to invite and how you will organize them, you need to determine how you will navigate the participants' busy schedules to find a time where everyone can be part of the discussion. Where will you hold the focus group meetings? Will you need to offer incentives to get people to participate? While it may not be feasible to pay participants like so many market research companies do, you can offer some sort of perk for the participants like dinner or refreshments—particularly if you are asking them to participate after a long day at work. When you plan for the actual focus group meeting or meetings, you need to be mindful to create a positive and comfortable setting in which to conduct them. You also want to make sure that the location you choose does not convey any sort of message regarding who is "in charge" in the inquiry process. For example, the parents you may want to invite may or may not feel comfortable coming into the school to talk about the school. They may be reluctant to discuss concerns while sitting in the middle of the school's media center or cafeteria. If this may be a potential problem, then you could consider a more neutral location in which to hold the focus group session or sessions.

Once you have planned for the logistics of your focus group, you then need to develop your questions. We suggest generating ten questions for your focus group and plan on the group discussing those questions for a time period of one and a half to two hours. Develop your questions according to four purposes (see Table 5.1). First, create at least one opening question that will allow all individuals to introduce themselves and feel comfortable talking in the group. If you ask them to share something about themselves with the opening question it also allows participants to see what they have in common with others in the group. Second, generate at least one introductory question. This question should ask for a general response to the overall topic of the group session and thus helps the group to start focusing on the

Table 5.1.
Focus Group Questions

Type of Question	# Per Group	Sample Question
Opening	1	Please share your name and your connection with Urban Heights Elementary School.
Introductory	1–2	You all passed the playground as you entered the building. What were your general impressions of the playground?
Transition	1–2	What are your personal feelings about recess?
Key	2–5	Given your impressions about recess and the general state of the playground, what do you think we should consider as top priorities for that area?
Closing	1	During our discussion I heard four top priorities and three major concerns. Have I missed anything?

topic. Following the introductory question, you should have a transition question or two. Once you know something about the participants and how they generally feel about the topic, then you want to try to connect the participants more specifically to the topic of the discussion group. Transition questions should help accomplish this. The majority of the focus group will focus on two to five key questions that follow your transition question. These questions will seek more specific information about the topic you are exploring. While the opening, introductory, and transition questions will probably take only five minutes each to explore, key questions should provide room for ten to fifteen minutes of discussion for each. These questions will be the most important sources of the data you will later analyze. Finally, you will also want to plan for an ending question. Ending questions bring the discussion to an end. You may choose to end your focus group by asking the group their overall opinions in terms of everything they have considered. You may also want to summarize what you have heard and ask the group if the summary is adequate. You may also choose to ask the group whether you have missed anything over the course of the discussion. Any of these choices provide an opportunity for the group to add final thoughts.

Using Interviews

There may be times when you are unable to pull together a team of stakeholders for a focus group, or you may have a sensitive topic to discuss and feel that individuals may not be as open in a focus group for fear of what others might think of them. You may also want to focus on the different perspectives people may have, and you may feel that if they are in a group they may be less likely to offer different views. In each of these instances you could still gather information by using one-on-one interviews. Like focus groups, interviews can provide valuable information regarding individual's perceptions, feelings, or experiences. Unlike focus groups, interviewers may feel more anonymous in a one-on-one situation, so they may feel like they can speak more candidly.

The interview process is much like the focus group. You are planning and facilitating a deliberate conversation in order to learn something. Like focus groups, you need to be very deliberate in selecting individuals to interview. You want to select a reasonable number to interview in hopes that you will get a good representation of views and perspectives. You also want to make sure you choose a good variety of individuals that represent diverse views and perspectives. For example, if you want to explore the effectiveness of lines of communication in you school and how that influences policy implementation and only interview team leaders, then you will, in all likelihood, get a very one-sided view of the subject. You also want to make sure you do not ask too many people. If you start to hear the same information over and over again, then you have saturated your data and do not need to continue interviewing individuals. While saturating data is not a problem in and of itself, you want to be mindful of your stakeholders' time and involvement. If you ask them to do an interview now that you may not need, they may be less likely to be interviewed or participate in a focus group about another issue at a later date.

Before you conduct your interviews you will need to develop a protocol of questions. When conducting multiple interviews about the same topic, you want to have the same list of questions for each interviewee. As you write your questions you need to keep in mind your audience. Word your questions in a way that you know they will understand. This is particularly important when you are interviewing children and individuals whose native language is not English. Also, make sure you are not using language that might bias your interviewee. For example, if you want to find out how teachers feel about the extracurricular experiences in their school, you would not ask, "Aren't all the hours you have to put in for these extra clubs draining?" Your interview questions should be designed for open-ended responses. If you pose questions that seek a "yes" or "no" answer, that is all you will get. It is better to pose questions asking for examples or degrees to which a person has an opinion and why. It is also helpful to ask a participant to describe an experience he or she has had and then use follow-up questions to help the participant interpret or analyze the experience. You will also want to be careful and avoid asking questions that the participant cannot answer. While this may happen unexpectedly, any question that throws the participant off-guard or where the participant does not have an answer may compromise his or her openness or general responsiveness for future questions. Occasionally during the interview, it may be helpful to recap what you have heard the participant say to make sure you are hearing it correctly. This also gives the participant an opportunity to elaborate on something he or she may have said previously.

Much like the focus group, you will want to have a question or two that helps the participant get comfortable talking while being recorded. The same format suggested for focus groups (omitting the opening question since it is only one person)—introduction, transition, key questions, and closing questions—is also appropriate within an interview. It is always good to offer a time at the end of the interview for the participant to share anything that he or she was not able to share based on the previous questions.

To ensure the best results, conduct your interview in a comfortable setting with as little distraction as possible. We strongly encourage you to tape-record the interview and transcribe it later. It is difficult to juggle asking questions, thinking about necessary follow-up questions, and recording information. Because you are using a tape recorder, you will want to avoid coffee shops and other locations where the background noise will get in the way of hearing the recording later. You may even have the interviewee suggest a location to make sure it is a comfortable setting for him or her. Before beginning the interview, you should thank the participant, explain why you are conducting the interview, and describe the format of the interview, including how long you expect it to take. In addition, you should remind the person that his or her response will be confidential—that you will always code the person's responses with a pseudonym in your notes and in any sort of report that follows. Also before you begin, you will want to give the participant a chance to ask questions about the interview itself.

Following the interview we strongly suggest that you follow up with an acknowledgment to the participant—a note in the mail thanking him or her will convey your appreciation for the person's time. Also, transcribe or have the interview transcribed as soon as possible following the interview and let the participant review the transcript for corrections or in the event that he or she wants something deleted. Once you have your interviews transcribed, you will have a rich source of data to examine in relation to the topic at hand. We will discuss using the data later in this chapter.

Using Surveys

A final source of data we want to suggest is surveys. Surveys can be helpful if you want to get the views or opinions from your entire school community. They are also helpful when you are trying to identify areas of focus for school improvement. For example, you may have brainstormed a number of areas of concern for your school: the playground, the food served at lunch, scheduling, and school safety. However, when you survey parents, you find that they are also more concerned about the amount of homework their children are bringing home every night. They do not seem to be concerned about school lunches. These results may change what you pursue first in any sort of school inquiry project. You may start with a focus group to discuss homework and wait to tackle the lunchroom.

On the surface, surveys may appear to be quicker and easier to use than focus groups or interviews. Do not be fooled by outward appearances. Good surveys take time, energy, and often financial resources in order to design and administer them effectively. Planning for a survey is critical because there is no way to correct poorly written questions or add questions you realize you should have asked once the survey has been administered.

If you determine that a survey is the best means through which you will get the information you need, then you need to begin by determining the purpose of the survey. What do you hope to learn from it? Stating your purpose will help put limits on the kinds of questions you ask. Often when people develop surveys, they ask too many questions. You want to make sure you get surveys returned. The longer they are, the less likely individuals will respond. Try to limit your survey to no more than twenty or twenty-five questions or statements, and try to keep them focused on a limited topic so the respondent does not have to mentally jump from one idea to another while completing the survey.

When designing your questions, you want to avoid asking for yes or no responses. While this gives you some information, it is still very limited. For example, if you want to know whether parents think a playground is safe enough and you ask, "Is the school's playground safe?" You may get 47 percent that say yes and 53 percent that say no. Of those respondents, some may be thinking, "Well, the chains on the swings are rusty, but that doesn't make it really unsafe, so I'll say 'yes,'" while others may think, "Those chains are rusty, so I guess I should say 'no.'" In both cases the respondents have very similar concerns, but you will not be able to tease that out according to your results. For all you know the yes's you receive are strong votes of confidence in the playground and the no's are individuals who want the playground shut down. In order to avoid this, we strongly suggest that you generate statements instead of questions and then provide a Likert scale of response choices. Likert scales typically offer respondents five choices: strongly agree, agree, neither agree nor disagree, disagree, and strongly disagree. By using a Likert scale, you have a better sense of your sample's feelings about an issue. Given the previous example, if you ask, "Overall, I believe the playground is a safe place for my children to play," and you get 12 percent who strongly agree, 18 percent who agree, 31 percent who neither agree nor disagree, 36 percent who disagree, and 3 percent who strongly disagree, you have a better sense of how the respondents recognize some issues with the playground that need to be addressed.

Once you have designed your questions, you will want others to review them. You may even want to run a pretest where you ask a group of individuals other than your intended sample to complete the survey and then see their results and hear feedback from them. This will help you determine whether your questions are written clearly and whether they give you the information you want. Again, we want to emphasize that an ounce of prevention is critical in surveys. If you do not catch problems during the planning stage, you will have to live with them after you have administered the survey.

Once you have designed your survey, you need to determine who should receive it and how they should receive it. You want to make sure your sample is large enough to represent your stakeholders—keeping in mind that you will not receive all of the surveys back. Determining sample size can be a challenging matter. Sample size will depend largely on how much confidence you will have in the responses you get—how likely is it that the information you got from the respondents actually represents the feelings of your overall stakeholders. You also want to consider the likelihood of return. If it is less likely that a large number of respondents will return the surveys, then you will need to increase your sample size. As a school, you do have some advantages. You can count on a fairly high return rate if you administer a survey to students during the school day. In addition, many schools will administer surveys on parent conference days while parents are waiting to meet with teachers. If you are able to plan for controlled situations, then you will have a higher return rate and may possibly need a smaller sample size. Particularly if a survey is a significant part of your data collection, you will want to make sure you have an adequate sample. To do this, you may choose to use a resource such as a random sample calculator. You can access one of these at the CustomInsight Web site: http://www.custominsight.com/articles/random-sample-calculator.asp.

Once you have determined your questions and your sample, you need to determine the best way to administer your survey. As we mentioned previously, using parent conference times to administer a survey is a good choice if most of the parents attend. However, if you have a significant number of parents who do not attend, or if you have a specific population of parents who do not attend (i.e., non-English-speaking parents who may not be able to get off from work to come) then your results will not represent a critical element of your school population if you administer it when they cannot respond. Similarly, if you choose to administer the survey through e-mail, you may only get parents and community members to respond who have access to the Internet in their homes. This would prevent your more economically challenged stakeholders from having their voices heard. You may have to determine multiple ways to administer the survey—parent conferences and/or e-mail for some stakeholders, and visits to housing projects, apartment buildings, or community centers for others.

Another critical element of planning for a survey involves planning for the results. If you wait until the surveys are returned, you may be overwhelmed by the data. We suggest you develop a database—usually Excel worksheets will suffice—and prepare yourself for the returned surveys. If you do this, you will be able to record the results as they come in and this will enable you to analyze the data much sooner. Hopefully you will include one or two open-ended questions along with your survey, in which case you need to determine the best way to record those responses as well.

Once you have completed the extensive planning, you are ready to administer your survey. It is critical that you make it very easy for participants to respond and return their responses. If you are mailing the surveys, be sure to include a stamped return envelope for respondents to return them. If you are sending the survey by e-mail, send a reminder or follow-up e-mail that thanks those who have responded and reminds others to respond. If you are administering it at school during a parent conference day, make sure the area where the survey is given provides plenty of pens or pencils and comfortable space to sit and respond. You may want to have the surveys available wherever parents sit and wait for their conference time. Also, if you are administering it at the school, make sure you have convenient drop-off boxes or sites for parents, so they do not have to go out of their way to return them. If you are administering the survey at a community center or a housing project, you could provide snacks or goodies as an incentive to draw people in to complete the survey. Any efforts you make along these lines are going to help increase the return rate for your survey.

When the surveys are returned, you will have a tremendous task ahead of you to record the responses. We would suggest designating someone as the recorder and offering some incentive or extra time for that individual to enter the data. You may have a parent volunteer who could do this. It would be a way for someone with data entry experience to help the school in a very meaningful way.

Steps for Using Surveys

✎ Establish purpose

✎ Generate questions/statements

✎ Pretest instrument

✎ Determine sample population

✎ Determine how to administer survey

✎ Prepare for data collection

✎ Administer survey

✎ Record survey results

✎ Analyze survey results

THE SUBJECT OF INQUIRY: ASKING THE RIGHT KINDS OF QUESTIONS

We have spent a fairly significant amount of time outlining ways you can collect data in your schools and community. It is equally important that we address the potential subjects about which you would collect data. Most of what we see about data in schools involves student achievement. In fact, most of the resources you will find about data-based decision making in schools solely look at student achievement data as defined by standardized test scores. We cannot emphasize strongly enough that simply looking at student achievement based on standardized test scores will not help you make authentic decisions about your school and community. Your school is a complex system influenced by many, many factors. It is essential that you ask questions that respond to that complexity if you really want to bring about meaningful and sustainable change.

Inquiry into Resources: Data about Teachers

As we have noted previously, teachers are a school's most vital and complex resource. As such, you need to invest time, energy, and financial resources into learning more about your teachers: why they accept their positions, why they stay, why they leave, how they feel about their work, how they feel about themselves, etc. Particularly in schools where teacher turnover is high and/or teacher morale appears to be low, it is professionally and morally inexcusable to neglect researching the quality of their work lives and the degree to which they feel connected and prepared.

While it would be impossible to list every potential line of inquiry a school could explore in relation to its teachers, we can suggest guidelines that may help stakeholders within a school community to discern potential directions of their inquiry about their teachers. These suggestions are not meant to be all-inclusive or prescriptive. Instead, they are mere suggestions to help stakeholders begin the important conversations that should lead them to increased levels of understanding about their school and its teachers.

One suggestion we have is to first identify, organize, and use the information you already have in order to determine what additional information you want or need. One simple teaching strategy that a number of teachers use is something called a KWL chart—What do we know? What do we want to know? What have we learned? The same framework fits nicely into an inquiry process. What do you know about your teachers? Often the school profile will include information such as years of experience and degrees for teachers. If the profile for the school or the district does not offer turnover rates, it should be fairly simple to track them—depending on access to previous profiles. What other untapped sources of data about teachers may be available? How about patterns of work? If the school has a sign-in/sign-out sheet, what can you learn about the hours teachers work? If your school has a professional library, how many and how often do teachers use it?

Once you are able to gather the data that already exists and examine it, then you may find points within the data that make you curious. You might notice trends of increased or decreased teacher turnover. You may also see shifts in the number of teachers who are seeking advanced degrees. Hopefully the initial data you gathered, coupled with what you have expressed as your purpose or mission, will lead you to ask additional questions and find other avenues through which you can collect data about your teachers.

Inquiry into Structure: Using Organizational Analysis to Better Understand Your School

Because schools are complex learning organizations, you can learn a great deal about them through thoughtful organizational analysis. Organizations are more than the sum of their parts. As we have shown in previous chapters, decisions are made with numerous possible responses. Dynamics exist within our schools based upon a number of organizational factors: degree of formalization in policies and procedures, lines of communication and decision making, organization of workload, and potential for collaboration are just a few that could be considered.

The formalization within a school deals with the degree to which specific policies and procedures are in place to control what happens—how people handle specific events or go about making decisions (or more accurately, the degree to which they can make decisions). When determining the level of formalization within your school, you can consider the following. Do teachers have specific formats and procedures they must follow in order to have a special event (e.g., grandparents' day) in their classrooms? When grade levels or committees meet, do they have to complete specific minutes and turn them into the office to be filed? Do teachers have to use specific templates for their lesson plans and then submit them weekly to someone for review? All of these examples point to a more highly formalized school. In contrast, your school may function more organically—where teachers operate with relative autonomy and are relatively free to explore special activities or initiatives without filling out paperwork or going through formal approval processes. Levels of formalization—particularly if that formalization compromises relationships for the sake of function—can significantly influence how teachers feel about their work as well as how they work. According to researchers, overly formalized organizations can lead to low employee morale, high levels of absenteeism, and high turnover rates among other concerns. Given the potential impact for overly formalized settings, it is important for you to examine the policies and procedures within your school to determine the degree to which they do or do not help people build relationships and grow professionally.

Somewhat related yet worthy of separate consideration, it is important to examine how information is transmitted and how decisions are made within your school. Often problems emerge within schools because lines of communication break down. In addition to very practical concerns regarding consistent implementation of policies, poor communication within a school can compromise a shared sense of purpose. When purpose is lost, tasks appear disjointed and arbitrary and stakeholders can feel lost or disconnected in the fray of activity.

In addition, the source of decision making can significantly influence a school in terms of compliance, morale, and a general sense of professionalism. The distance between the source of a decision and the source of implementation will significantly influence employee perception and organizational dynamics. Consider how teachers in your building respond when they are told by their district office to implement a program developed by some team of experts far, far removed. They are being directed by individuals removed from their situations to implement something created by an even more distant authority. Whether teachers visibly resent the district directives or not, over time these impositions will take their toll. Particularly when decision making is removed to a higher authority on a regular basis, teachers may very well lose faith in themselves to make their own professional judgments or they may lose the skill sets (or for younger teachers, may never develop skill sets) to make meaningful decisions about curriculum and instruction.

The same concerns can emerge when a principal or administrative team makes all the decisions within a school. Teachers do not develop capacities to exercise professional judgments for themselves. Compare the potential situation with a teacher who authoritatively controls her classroom versus a teacher who teaches her children to take responsibility for their actions. If any of you have ever served as a substitute teacher, then you can spot the difference immediately. When the authoritative teacher is absent, the classroom falls apart because the students do not know how to make good choices on their own. In contrast, in the latter classroom where a teacher has empowered her students to make good choices, often a day with a substitute teacher operates just as smoothly as when the teacher is there. With these images in mind, you can see how examining lines of communication and sources of decision making can reveal significant challenges and opportunities within a school seeking change.

In addition to formalization and lines of communication/decision making, we encourage you to consider workload and the state of collaboration within your school. How does your school utilize its personnel points? Does the distribution of work support the stated mission of your school? Does the school rely on traditional images of how to organize personnel within a school, and, as a result, miss out on opportunities to work differently? How do stakeholders within your school work together? Do committees and teams have adequate time to engage in meaningful collaboration? Does your school have so many initiatives that you have little time to reflect on the decisions you have made and deliberately consider future directions? The accumulated knowledge and energy of stakeholders within a school community is a valuable resource. It is vital that schools take time to make sure the knowledge and energy of its teachers, staff, parents, and community members is used in meaningful and productive ways.

Inquiry into Culture: Looking Closely at Your Environment

The culture of a school includes the rules (written and unwritten), values, and relationships that influence how individuals behave, think, and feel about their organization and themselves within that organization. A school's culture includes such relational elements as trust, empathy, self-efficacy, and motivation. One way you could study the culture of your school would involve looking at how individuals feel about the school and their roles there. This line of inquiry would shed light on one level of the school's culture. You could also investigate the collective sentiments about the school, its level of morale, etc. Seeking greater understanding of group dynamics and how the school and community influence those dynamics could certainly provide valuable insights as you attempt to bring about change in your school.

If the school's culture seems to be a critical area of concern and the focus of much of your inquiry project, then you may want to explore it in multiple ways—including a focus on the school's cultural capital. Cultural capital includes the social resources individuals or groups possess that give them advantages over others. These advantages can appear in many forms—social, informational, and political to name just a few. Social capital influences the kinds of relationships people are able to develop and sustain. Think about the various cliques in your school community. These social groups may include teachers, parents, or community members. What advantages do they have by virtue of their association with one another? Do they get information before others? Do they have connections that other people in the community do not? Do they have the ear of key decision makers and as a result tend to get their way? In addition to using social connections, some in your organization may have advantages because they have information others do not. Think about the parent who enters an Individualized Education Plan (IEP) meeting for his or her child and hears a barrage of acronyms with no understanding of their meaning. That parent typically sits quietly and does not challenge what is being said by the "experts."

Inquiry into Context: Connecting with Your Community through Heightened Understanding

The final suggestion regarding potential inquiry projects is the context in which the school functions—the school community. No organization is an island—least of all schools. It is particularly critical to study the community when schools, as this book suggests, are striving to involve all stakeholders. Much like we suggested when we discussed studying teachers, we believe a great deal of information about your community already exists. You should be able to access information about your school's community from a variety of sources: U.S. Census Bureau, community Web sites, local libraries, and Chambers of Commerce. Generating a basic profile is a good starting place for an inquiry project dealing with the school community. Again, as we addressed previously when planning for inquiry for teachers, the KWL process might help stakeholders determine possible avenues to explore in the local community—both for its needs and its resources.

CONCLUSION: SUSTAINED UNDERSTANDING DOES NOT COME CHEAPLY

As you can see from all the potential avenues for inquiry we have introduced in this chapter, engaging in inquiry projects like this take tremendous commitment and resources. Data-based school reform cannot be done cheaply and it cannot be done on top of everything else people are expected to do in the reform initiative culture of today. If you do not invest time and resources into your inquiry projects, then you will send a message to your stakeholders that it is really not very important.

How do you secure resources to support inquiry projects within your school? One way you can find financial resources is to apply for research grants. We recommend seeking sources through a Web site, http://www.teacherscount.org. This site provides links to over fifty grants and financial awards for teachers. In addition, a number of professional associations such as the National Council for Teachers of Mathematics (NCTM), National Middle School Association (NMSA), Kappa Delta Pi, and the National Parent Teacher Association also offer small grants that can help support school research. Universities and State agencies, and state-level professional associations also have funds for schools and individual teachers. While it may take some time to search for these sources, finding them and securing funds from them will help you in your efforts, so it is time well invested.

Even if you are able to secure additional funds, you will still need to plan for the necessary supports in order to increase the likelihood that your efforts will be successful. While you may not be able to financially compensate teachers for participation, but you can write up the work so they can earn district-level professional development credit for their efforts.

Partnerships with area universities may also bring needed support through teacher leadership preparation and research. We encourage you to go to universities with proposals for partnerships that extend beyond the typical student–teacher placement. These partnerships could include internships, inviting university researchers in to do research in the school with you, creating new opportunities for field experiences, etc.

You should also consider ways to take advantage of the resources within your community. As we mentioned early in this book, schools in urban areas have significant resources nearby. We challenge you to rethink the movement toward corporate partners who provide goodies for teacher appreciation or small tokens and instead strategically find partners who can help you develop and sustain meaningful inquiry projects for sustainable school improvement. Your parents may also be another vital resource in this work. Whether they have experience and expertise in research and data analysis or not, you can invite them to the planning and training of your inquiry projects and use them as researchers in your school. You send a powerful message to the parents and community members in your school community when you invite them in to help you better understand your own school and community. You tell them that you have nothing to hide and that you need their commitment and support in order to bring about change.

Finally, we will make a suggestion that may seem radical to some. If you are really committed to data-driven change within your school—gathering substantive data about your teachers, culture, structure, and community— then you need to place a moratorium on other new initiatives in order to do this well. All new initiatives take time and resources to implement, and as we noted previously, many schools find themselves adopting more and more initiatives even though they have no history of successfully implementing any of them. While it may take tremendous courage and political clout to stand up and say, "No new initiatives for the next two to three years," we believe it may be the most important stand you could take for your school. We encourage you to use data to support your position. Your argument may sound something like the following:

> In the past five years we have started nine new initiatives, and to date, we have no evidence that any of them have been implemented successfully. Therefore, we are going to take a step back, gather meaningful data about our school, develop more collaborative relationships with our stakeholders, and then determine where to go next.

You can also point to businesses as models—showing that they do not make changes without thoroughly researching the implications. You can also make a financial argument for the moratorium. Funds that would be spent supporting the implementation of new initiatives could be used, instead, for your inquiry projects. Further, time that would be spent in professional development to implement the initiatives could also be used to support your research. We encourage you to use your parents and community members to support your position. They can apply pressure to district administration and school boards in ways that you cannot. They do not have to worry about threats to job security or other repercussions because they are not employed by the school district.

To conclude this section of the book specifically directed to teachers, administrators, and other school personnel, we have suggested extensive work in the form of inquiry projects—gathering data about the school that goes beyond the pervasive standardized test score data used exclusively by most schools and districts. Until you start to collect the kind of data that brings meaning to your school as a complex system, you will be forced to react to simplistic judgments about your work. Without a deeper understanding of your school, you will not be able to bring about meaningful and sustainable change. Without meaningful data to back you up, you will be unable to fight for the changes you need to make within your school and your community.

How to Support Inquiry Projects in Your School

- Seek funding through grants
- Partner with universities
- Take advantage of community resources
- Involve parents in data collection and analysis
- Place a moratorium on other initiatives

REFERENCES

CustomInsight.com.(2007). *Random Sampling Overview*, http://www.custominsight. com/articles/random-sampling.asp. Retrieved December 21, 2007.

Johnson, R. and Waterfield, J. (2004). Making words count: The value of qualitative research. *Physiotherapy Research International*, 9(3), 121–131.

Krueger, R. and Casey, M. (2000). *Focus Groups: A Practical Guide for Applied Research*. 3rd ed. Thousand Oaks, CA: Sage Publications.

Peterson, E. R. and Barron, K. A. (2007). How to get focus groups talking: New ideas that will stick. *International Journal of Qualitative Methods*, 6(3), 140–145.

Yorgason, D. (2007). *Research and Development Activities of U.S. Multinational Companies: Preliminary Results from the 2004 Benchmark Study*. Washington, DC: Bureau of Economic Analysis, http://www.bea.gov/scb/pdf/2007/ 03March/0307RDofMNCs.pdf. Retrieved December 21, 2007.

PART III

A Critical Conversation for Parents and Community Members

CHAPTER 6

Politics and Policies: Beginning the Conversation

There is a pervasive belief among parents and citizens across the country that urban schools have always been a problem, with gangs, drug abuse, teen pregnancies, and poor test scores evident in every inner-city school. Mostly populated by lower class children of color, it is thought that middle-class parents avoid sending their children to these supposedly disorganized chaotic schools where little learning takes place. While this is the current image of urban schools, educational historian John Rury contends that at one time urban schools were role models for the rest of the country and that was less than a half-century ago. At that time, city schools had greater resources, wider range of courses, with better paid teachers. With special curriculum, these schools attracted gifted students. They were both good and bad urban schools at one time—or so it seemed. But by 1988, then Secretary of Education, William Bennett, labeled Chicago's urban schools as the worst in the nation, and other urban areas also were painted with the same brush. The Carnegie Foundation's report of 1988 also echoed Bennett's concern, labeling all urban schools "human storehouses."

So, what changed for urban schools between 1958 and 1988? Even though the Great Migration of Blacks northward had slowed by this time, court-ordered desegregation, however, had fueled middle-class fears about crime and deteriorating urban schools and neighborhoods. Couple those conditions with huge waves of immigrants from Mexico, Central America, and the Caribbean arriving in the 80s and urban schools were ripe to serve as the fulcrum point for the public's discontent with the American educational system. Of Spanish descent, these Hispanic students represent the fastest growing student group in the nation's public schools. They pose a huge challenge for urban educators who were also dealing with long-standing issues of inner-city poverty and racial segregation. Not only do Hispanics now constitute the fastest growing minority in schools, they also present the lowest educational achievement data and the highest dropout rates.

Urban communities have also been dramatically impacted by the growing middle-class suburbs, which have helped to create poor inner city cores. They are racially isolated with the wealth of the community spread out into surrounding suburban areas of white enclaves. Once the federal government interceded with desegregation plans, the stage was set for other players to become involved in reshaping the urban school. This chapter tells the story of how national school reform has greatly impacted urban education and what the lessons are for parents in understanding the Etch-a-Sketch of school reform in twenty-first-century urban schools.

CULTURAL COMBATANTS

At the Republican National Convention in 1992, conservative politician Pat Buchanan declared that religious groups were fighting over the soul of America. This politician was adding his own spin on an increasingly acrimonious public debate over which competing cultural and moral values were of most worth for public education in the United States. This battle had been brewing in education for some time, represented by the curriculum wars on both coasts of the country. Eventually, the standards movement, capped by the federal law No Child Left Behind would soon be a part of this national debate over what education could and should be for all students.

In the mid-1980s, the National Endowment for the Humanities funded an assessment of history and literature knowledge among seventeen-year-olds conducted by the National Assessment of Educational Progress (NAEP). The results were published in a book, *What Do Our 17-Year-Olds Know?* (1987), written by Diane Ravitch and Chester Finn, who argued that the test data proved that the younger generation is culturally illiterate, who could only read or write except at the most rudimentary level, with virtually no knowledge except that conveyed through the television set. While the overall results of the assessment were open to interpretation, many specific findings were easily sensationalized, lending credence to claims that young people lacked basic cultural knowledge.

Other conservatives also supported Ravitch and Finn. In his popular book *Cultural Literacy*, E. D. Hirsch (1987) argued that learning a core body of shared knowledge was especially important in an increasingly diverse society, and he included in his book a list of what literate Americans know. Another conservative, Allan Bloom (1987), lamented *The Closing of the American Mind* by such a poor educational system.

The writings of Bloom, Ravitch, Finn, and Hirsch—bolstered by the political rhetoric of Pat Buchanan, the religious right, and the eventual national celebrity of radio personality Rush Limbaugh and Republican Congressman Newt Gingrich—helped to heighten public awareness about educational reform terminology such as school restructuring, standards, and accountability. This national attention helped move such ideas forward as public policy attempted to deal both with the growing diversity of the American population and the public educational system's inability to effectively deal with that diversity, especially in urban centers. Unlike earlier periods of school reform, however, the symbolic value of winning the culture wars would be very much in play in the curriculum wars as the standards movement unfolded throughout the 1990s.

BI-COASTAL CURRICULUM WARS

Primarily fought in states with large immigrant populations, the 1990s curriculum wars were waged over what it means to be "American," as well as how the history of America should be taught. Throughout the 1980s and 1990s, California absorbed nearly half of all new legal and illegal immigrants, while New York, Florida, and Texas gained the majority of the rest of the newcomers. By 1993, a Gallup poll reported that 65 percent of Americans were ready to stop the flow of immigrants because of the increasing demands placed on the infrastructures of these four states, particularly the capacities of their public school systems.

California symbolized how the nation was changing during this time. Faced with huge numbers of English as a second language (ESL) students and not enough teachers who could speak the different languages and dialects represented in the state's schools, Bill Honig, the state's superintendent of education, orchestrated the reform of each grade's curriculum frameworks. Adopted by the California state board in 1987 (and reaffirmed in 1997), this curriculum framework attempts to create a blend of nationalism and pluralism by asserting that America is a land of immigrants who share common values and ideals, and that these common standards unite the country, representing an American culture created by many groups of immigrants. While educational historian Diane Ravitch asserted that the framework stressed the racial and ethnic diversity of the country through intergroup respect, other scholars such as Catherine Cornbleth and Christine Sleeter disagreed.

But these analyses occurred after the fact, for it was not until public debate over state-adopted textbooks erupted that the California curriculum framework earned careful scrutiny. With textbooks reflecting the state's History-Social Science framework in hand, women, people of color, and other minorities voiced concerns about their exclusion from the books under consideration. The 1990 California textbook controversy developed in tandem with a growing national debate about the "American identity." Ravitch wrote extensively about the negative impact that multiculturalism could have on school children, authoring nine pieces of published work in 1990 alone about school curriculum. As California fought its own curriculum war, the stage was set on the country's east coast for yet another national curriculum controversy.

In contrast to California's view of the great melting pot, New York's educational leaders had a different perspective, thus creating a different type of curriculum of inclusion. Both educators and employers in New York had determined that non-whites, who made up a growing percentage of the work force, were not doing as well as children of European descent on "almost every standardized test used in the New York public school system. In response to this crisis of confidence in education, New York Commissioner of Education, Thomas Sobol, convened a task force charged with reviewing the social studies syllabi and instructional materials reflected the pluralistic nature of American society.

After completing its review, the task force issued its report, "A Curriculum of Inclusion," identifying a systematic bias toward European culture in state curriculum materials and, with strong rhetoric, denounced this bias as representing institutionalized racism. Supporting the task force's recommendations, Commissioner Sobol noted a pattern of failure that was directly associated with race and poverty of the students from the cities and rural areas. Believing that the system had failed the students who are poor and in minority, Sobol's plans were supported by the state's School Boards Association and the New York City Board of Education, though not by conservatives like Ravitch and historian Arthur Schlesinger.

Under the watchful eyes of his critics, Sobol next formed a social studies syllabus review and development committee made up of a panel of education scholars who were charged with examining the twenty-year-old state social studies curriculum and recommending changes in its content and use, with the goal of improving students' understanding of one another, American culture, and the world at large. In the summer of 1991, the committee issued its advisory report, "One Nation, Many Peoples: A Declaration of Cultural Interdependence," suggesting that the New York social studies syllabi be revised to provide more opportunities for students to learn from multiple perspectives and that racist or sexist language be removed. They also advocated a shift from the mastery of information to the development of intellectual processes, with an emphasis on depth, not breadth, and on critical thinking rather than on memory of isolated facts.

At the core of these curriculum wars lay the question of whether and how to use multiculturalism as a lens to improve teaching, student learning, and education in general. One historian of the period, Jonathan Zimmerman, contends that by 1996, the "culture wars" became almost synonymous with the struggle over multiculturalism in the classroom. Historians and conservatives alike seemed more interested in preserving the status quo (or "maintaining the nation" as they phrased it) in the face of a rapidly growing immigrant population that was increasingly labeled "at-risk" by a national report, *A Nation at Risk*, which ultimately united politicians and businessmen into claiming control over the country's public education system.

A Nation at Risk represented the culminating effort of the National Commission on Excellence in Education, and signaled the development of new priorities for the federal government's approach to education reform. Striking in its charged rhetoric, the report equated the state of education in the United States to an "act of war" and made direct comparisons between the economic competitiveness of the U.S. economy and other countries, particularly Japan, South Korea, and Germany. Additionally, the report cited a number of "indicators of risk" that included declining SAT scores, low student scores in literacy, science and math, and poor showings on international comparisons of student achievement. The authors placed the blame for these shortcomings on incompetent teachers and lazy students. This report, however, simmered in the nation's consciousness and along with William Bennett denouncing Chicago's urban schools and President Reagan's attempt to dismantle the United States Department of Education, by the late 1980s, the time had come for politicians to claim school reform for their own political games.

THE ETCH-A-SKETCH OF NATIONAL EDUCATION REFORM

On September 27, 1989, President George H. W. Bush, the self-declared "education president," met with forty-nine of the nation's governors for a two-day education summit at the University of Virginia in Charlottesville. With Arkansas Governor Bill Clinton serving as summit cochair, the group set about the task of establishing, for the first time, national education goals. The summit represented a shift in the focus of school reform efforts, as politicians from both political parties deliberately turned their attention away from such issues as school funding and equal access and toward educational outcomes and accountability.

The general feeling at the education summit was that despite grave concerns announced in *A Nation at Risk*, little had been accomplished in terms of student achievement. In a final press release, conference participants stressed the need for creating a "system of accountability" and called for more systematic reporting of school, district, and state performance, increased parental choice, school-based management, and alternative certification for teachers. Thus, President George H. W. Bush's education summit represents a pivotal turning point because it links the politically driven but essentially unmandated *A Nation at Risk* of 1983 to the legal enactment of national education policy that culminated in President George W. Bush's *No Child Left Behind Act* of 2001.

Shortly after the publication of *A Nation at Risk*, the National Governors' Association (NGA), meeting in August 1985, created seven task forces to study and report on "tough questions" concerning education reform. Two of these governors, Lamar Alexander of Tennessee and Richard Riley of South Carolina, would go on to serve as U.S. Secretary of Education, Alexander under George H. W. Bush and Riley under Bill Clinton. In 1986, the NGA released its forward-looking report, *Time for Results: The Governors' 1991 Report on Education.* The task force on leadership and management, chaired by Arkansas Governor Bill Clinton, recommended that state governments create incentives that promoted school site management and improvement; collect statewide data on schools and student learning; and to offer reward to principals and schools for performance and effectiveness.

In addition to government intervention, corporate America's interest in school reform became quite pronounced, with business leaders gaining unprecedented levels of input into education policy. Indeed, President George W. Bush actively sought the support of corporate organizations like the Business Roundtable, challenging CEOs to get involved in school reform. With a membership of some 200 corporate leaders representing the nation's biggest companies, the Business Roundtable quickly took Bush up on his challenge by crafting a nine-point education initiative with which to lobby state legislatures and monitor state progress on school reform.

By the time, then, that the first President Bush and the nation's governors gathered for their education summit, many of the recommendations that would find their way into the school reform legislation of the 1990s had already been made. Concluding their meeting on September 28, 1989, they decided for the first time to establish *national education goals* that would "guarantee an internationally competitive standard" in six areas by the year 2000.

Goals 2000

The debate on national standards was elevated to policy level through a series of commissions and reports that began to appear following the creation in 1990 of the National Education Goals Panel (NEGP). Consisting of governors, members of congress, members of the president's administration and state legislators, the NEGP quickly recommended that Congress establish a National Council on Education Standards and Testing to study the feasibility of establishing national standards. *Raising Standards for American Education*, the report issued by this council, recommended creating a permanent body to approve national education standards.

In its own report, *Promises to Keep: Creating High Standards for American Students*, the group anticipated the creation of a permanent body, called the National Education Standards and Improvement Council (NESIC), as part of President Clinton's Goals 2000 legislation.

The resulting NESIC-certified national standards would then be available for use and adaptation by state governments as they developed their own content standards. In addition to being voluntary, the standards had to be academic, world-class, and useful and adaptable, as well as originating through bottom-up development characterized by a consensus building process that involves educators, parents, and community leaders from schools and neighborhoods across the country. Congress passed President Clinton's Goals 2000 in March 1994, formally creating the NESIC and setting the stage for the creation and certification of national curriculum standards.

From its inception, Goals 2000 proved to be controversial. Despite its origins in the first Bush administration, many conservatives felt that national education goals came perilously close to mandating national standards—an unacceptable intrusion on the part of the federal government into state and local matters. The promotion of national standards, even without a mandate, became a politically expedient way to symbolically address issues of accountability and to shift the public policy debate away from inputs—or the distribution of resources both in and out of schools—toward outputs that are used to distribute rewards and punishments for teachers and students. One of the apparent consequences of the national standards debate was that the national conversation around school reform, involving politicians and business people, was now slowly but steadily shifting toward systems of accountability used to reward and punish schools, teachers, and principals.

From National Goals to State Assessments: Educators Lose Control

Another aspect of President Clinton's education agenda in 1994 was state accountability. With passage of the Goals 2000 legislation in the spring of 1994, attention turned toward reauthorization of the Elementary and Secondary Education Act (ESEA), particularly Title I funds for compensatory education programs. This new law, the Improving America's Schools Act, reauthorized ESEA and for the first time, linked Title I grants to school reform efforts. This new legislation required states to construct school improvement and assessment plans based on state-developed content and performance standards in at least mathematics and reading. Progress toward meeting these standards was to be measured three times over the course of a student's school experience.

Since 1986, when the National Governors Association began to take the lead in promoting school reform efforts, many state governments had also become active in legislating various kinds of school reform initiatives. For example, spurred into action by a Kentucky State Supreme Court decision that found inequitable school funding to be in violation of the state constitution, that state's legislature passed the landmark 1990 Kentucky Education Reform Act. This act represented the most sweeping statewide reform effort at the time by equalizing state funding, creating a mechanism for school-based decision making, setting performance standards, and instituting a state-directed system of accountability that rewarded schools able to reach the standards and "sanctioned" those that did not.

The refinement of the 1990 Kentucky Education Reform Act illustrates how the focus of school accountability systems in the 1990s evolved from an initial concern with what Darling-Hammond and Ascher have called *professional* accountability to one that emphasized *bureaucratic* accountability. Bureaucratic accountability rests on procedural, top-down directives, whereas professional accountability requires teachers to make their own decisions concerning students, and therefore assumes a high level of competency and knowledge. Yet, as the 1990s wore on, the question of such school-based autonomy seemed to become lost as states enacted increasingly rigid accountability requirements grounded in bureaucratic management and governmental oversight in their quest for education reform and renewal.

THE ROAD TO A PEDAGOGY OF POVERTY

In 1998 the Center for Education Reform, the Thomas B. Fordham Foundation, Empower America, and the Heritage Foundation jointly sponsored an update to the original 1983 *Nation at Risk* report. This update, "A Nation Still at Risk," claimed that American schools were continuing to fail because the gap in the quality of schools was based on poverty and race. Citing these as moral reasons for change, the update offered two main renewal strategies—standards, assessments and accountability, and competition and choice—as the means to providing equal educational opportunity for all students.

By 2001, forty-nine states had developed versions of these strategic renewal strategies. Not only did virtually every state create its own educational standards, twenty-eight implemented state-mandated assessments, with seventeen states instituting promotion and retention standards based on these assessments. In the view of some, though, this "whips and chains" mentality, dependent upon standards-based assessment to determine which schools, which teachers, and which students achieve success, is one of the major drawbacks of current school reform.

McNeil convincingly documented the effects of such standardization in Houston, Texas, where the so-called "Texas miracle" began. The primary motivation, initially, for education reform was low teacher salaries. However, the appointment of billionaire businessman and presidential candidate H. Ross Perot to lead the state reform brought a corporate sensibility that valued quality control and a clear, measurable return on investment. The result was an education reform package that imposed a tightly controlled top-down structure of school and curriculum governance while still offering too few resources.

Touting the Texas miracle of improved public education, President George W. Bush signed into law the No Child Left Behind (NCLB) Act on January 8, 2002. As the first reauthorization of the ESEA since 1994, NCLB in many ways looked backward. The act disbanded the NEGP, which had been created during the administration of Bush's father and had, for more than a decade, been reporting on national progress toward the 2000 education goals. NCLB required states to use their own assessments in measuring reading and mathematics achievement in grades 3–8 and to use NAEP tests on a sample of 4th and 8th graders every other year. States were further required to demonstrate academic proficiency for all students within twelve years. Any school that was unable to make adequate progress for two years would be required to allow students to exercise an option for school choice and go elsewhere. Each year until 2014, an increasing percentage of students are required to demonstrate "proficiency." At that time in all states and in all schools every student (regardless of ability or proficiency, whether they have a disability or are recent immigrants to the United States) is expected to be proficient in every subject. In short, NCLB put the public education system on notice to perform or else, just as Ravitch had warned, they will forfeit their claim to public support.

Ironically, this law requires the use of instructional programs that are based upon "scientifically based research" yet there is no research that supports its major tenets of school choice, standards, corrective action or restructuring as major change agents in improving student achievement. In fact, Michael Casserly of the Council of the Great City Schools reported in 2007 that the law has no plan of action on exactly how to improve student learning. In essence, it has become a law of compliance rather than a law of results.

Moreover, the language of NCLB offers a particular view of knowledge by narrowing the curriculum which often leads to students learning less rather than more, and by presuming that standards have been objectively determined. This narrowing of the curriculum does not transfer well into the larger world beyond school and thus urban and disadvantaged students fall further behind. With more money spent on test-taking materials and less on enrichment, urban students are more likely to be forced out of school or retained before they must take the required exams, insuring that the test scores for their schools will hopefully reach adequate yearly progress (AYP).

Perhaps even more damaging to the parent–school relationship is the repeated contempt of teachers by such individuals as Hirsch who assert that teachers often mislead parents and that teachers fall prey to fads and untested curricula. As noted above, the law requires that schools that receive federal funds must choose "scientifically-based research" programs that are approved by the federal government.

Pedagogy of Poverty in Urban Schools

One dramatic consequence of the "Texas miracle" that became George W. Bush's NCLB educational centerpiece is an enhanced "teaching to the test" mentality with an overreliance on drill and practice, lecture, and rote learning as noted in McNeil's study of the Houston schools. Ironically, this kind of teaching and learning was identified nearly fifty years ago in Martin Haberman's studies of urban classrooms. Back then, Haberman found that teachers engaged in a typical format which constituted the core functions of instruction. Performed to the systematic exclusion of other instructional acts, Haberman was the first to label these actions as a "pedagogy of poverty."

Pedagogy of Poverty

Giving information	Giving tests
Asking questions	Reviewing tests
Giving directions	Settling disputes
Making assignments	Punishing noncompliance
Monitoring seatwork	Marking papers
Reviewing assignments	Giving grades

A pedagogy of poverty places the teacher in control of all classroom talk. With the overreliance on prefabricated curricular programs that seem to predominate in many urban schools with large, at-risk Title I populations, teachers must literally read scripted lessons to all students, eliminating the matching of instruction to the needs of individual students. Neither students nor teachers make pedagogical choices in these settings where students see their teachers as functionaries doing what the book tells them to do, and teachers are required to forego a democratic classroom wherein they create and facilitate dynamic and distinctive teaching–learning processes.

Haberman contends that this type of instruction appeals to people who believe that students have to be forced to learn and should not be allowed choices (a sign of permissiveness). Those who favor this type of instruction believe that schools exist to *transmit* knowledge, skills, and dispositions, and that students need to be controlled, especially those who are "at-risk" and lack the requisite learning skills and habits of the dominant culture. Inevitably, it is "at-risk" students who are most negatively affected by this type of instruction. Typically in the past, and ever-increasingly so now, many of these students are immigrants (or children of immigrants), and do not yet understand democratic principles.

Adopting a pedagogy of poverty in service to reform-mandated measures of standardization creates a system of "subtractive schooling" according to education scholar, Angela Valenzuela. It is one that separates or subtracts students from their teachers, their courses, their education and themselves. Learning becomes narrow, prescribed, and depersonalized. For children of recent immigrants in particular, it signals them to *not* conform to a U.S. school, for to do so is to chance losing one's cultural identity. Students are further distanced by a generic curriculum that is constructed in such a way that it can be tested and scored by a computer. With no relation to who they are and what they are interested in, standardized instruction and tests are recognized as good for the principal, or the school, or the teachers—but not for the student. McNeil further contends that the reform and standardization of Texas education (through the use of a pedagogy of poverty) have expanded the educational inequalities and disguised the historical and persistent inequities of the Texas public schools.

These inequities are exacerbated by this pedagogy of poverty used not only in Texas, but across the country, where we now know based on Swanson's research that at least seven out of ten entering ninth graders graduate. Graduation rates are even lower for students of color and lower still for students who attend urban high schools (only five out of ten graduate) in the fifty largest urban centers in the country. Gary Orfield, director of Harvard's Civil Rights Project, has called the drop-out rate not just a case of losing our future, but also a catastrophe ignored, but only until recently with the publication of the 2008 *Cities in Crisis*.

Other studies have found this type of pedagogy to be common in schools that serve large Hispanic populations with limited English language skills, and other minority students. The National Research Council has also reported grave assessments of various accountability systems. By 2000, two such reports had documented that the curricular decisions and accountability measures undertaken by school systems in Texas and Charlotte, North Carolina, had been detrimental for African American students (in both studies), even though some evidence of gains was noted in Texas for whites and Hispanics.

Jonathan Kozol has also documented this type of teaching in his visits to more than sixty urban schools where he found teaching materials were actually manuals or workbooks which were used to prime children into taking specific tests. Kozol also discovered that teachers in urban schools filled with black and Hispanic children are using a pro-military type of discipline with behavior control techniques found in prisons. Since this type of learning is barren of richness and uses robotic instructional methods, many educators and researchers believe that this pedagogy of poverty encourages passivity in students while stifling creativity, curiosity, and the development of critical thinking and problem solving skills.

But, according to Haberman there is good teaching and educators and parents can recognize it when they see the following occurring:

Good Pedagogy Involves Students

with issues they regard as vital concerns;

with explanations of human differences;

with major concepts, big ideas, and general principles and not isolated facts;

in planning what they will be doing;

applying ideals such as fairness, equity, or justice to their world;

doing things rather than watching, and just listening;

in real-life experiences;

in heterogeneous groups;

in thinking about an idea in ways that question common sense and the status quo and asks them to relate new ideas to old learning or to apply the idea to the problems of living;

redoing, polishing, or perfecting their own work;

reflecting on their own lives and how they have come to believe and feel as they do; and

they have teachers who involve them with the technology of information access.

As an example of the last tenet of good teaching, Songer, Lee, and Kam tracked classroom research on a technology-rich inquiry weather program with six urban science teachers using a district-wide science reform. In nineteen middle school classrooms, students were provided instruction that encouraged ownership and control of their learning and then demonstrated significant content and inquiry gains on the district's standardized tests. Their work documented that urban students and teachers were successful in programs that fostered inquiry learning for students in the classroom with accompanying professional development activities for the teachers which moved them away from using bad pedagogical practices. They found that technology-enriched instruction that was inquiry-based added relevance, student content and inquiry learning, enthusiasm and fluency in technology to the classroom. By recognizing that their ideas had value and worth, students' enthusiasm increased dramatically and they became excited about learning.

CLOSING THE GAP, TEST SCORES AND STUDENT LEARNING

NCLB uses standardized tests as the primary if not sole means to document the achievement of students and schools. As a result, many people involved with schools speak only of the test scores when they talk about their work in schools. They seem to forget the students who take the tests—so what is a standardized test score and what does it tell us about the student who took the test?

James Popham is a retired professor at UCLA; he is also a former test maker and a noted expert on educational testing. He says that standardized achievement tests are used by citizens and board members to evaluate a school's effectiveness, even though such tests should not be used to judge the quality of education. Students' scores on these tests reflect what is taught in school, as well as the student's intellectual ability and his or her out-of school learning opportunities. A student's socioeconomic status significantly influences test scores because so many test items on standardized achievement tests focus on assessing knowledge learned outside of school. Thus, poorer students are faced with a number of challenges in relation to testing. They typically have fewer educational opportunities within urban schools given the pedagogy of poverty described previously. Further, they tend to have the least-prepared teachers and fewer experiences outside of school that would help them do as well on standardized achievement tests as their middle-class suburban peers.

But test scores matter—and in urban schools, evidence suggests that teaching and learning are increasingly organized around these tests. Darling-Hammond and Rustique-Forrester found that in urban schools teachers are teaching to the low-level learning of multiple-choice standardized achievement tests. Rather than engaging students in extensive writing, critical thinking, and problem-solving activities needed to be successful in college and the workplace, teachers are choosing (or being forced to choose) to pass by enriched curriculum in order to prepare students for the tests. Darling-Hammond notes that the administration of NCLB has discouraged the use of other ways to teach and assess students—ways that encourage higher levels of thinking and learning that can be applied in meaningful ways in their lives. Instead, urban schools often rely on the standardized test scores and use them for determining grade retention and tracking.

As yet another example of misusing testing, Kozol found that students in the very first two years of schooling are spending at least two weeks of testing in the first two months of the school year. This process is known as "front-loading children" by educators across the country. The goal is supposedly to provide teachers with evidence of the children's weaknesses. Since most of these children come from lower income homes and are non-English speaking, they do not know how to read or how to hold a pencil, much less how to take a test. To make matters worse, nap-time, art, music, and physical education are often eliminated to accommodate this kind of testing.

Given the impact of federal legislation on public schools, many researchers have studied what test scores actually tell us about closing the gap between racial and income-based achievement groups and student learning. Darling-Hammond tells us that in the years following the Supreme Court decision of Brown in the mid-1950s, efforts were made at school finance reform to equalize school funding. We also know that President Johnson's War on Poverty increased investments in urban schools with gains made to help equalize educational opportunities. These efforts did make inroads in the gaps between poor and rich and black and white students through the mid-1980s. By the late 1980s, however, most of these federally sponsored program investments in college access programs for urban students were eliminated. At the same time, as noted above, the country absorbed the largest wave of immigrants since the 1890s—most of whom were poor Hispanics who did not speak English. Also, occurring almost simultaneously, childhood poverty rates and homelessness increased and lack of access to health care also grew. Exacerbated by the increased numbers of students requiring second language instruction and special education services, the achievement gap began to widen again, and under NCLB, it has continued. Furthermore, since many states have failed to invest in the education of inner-city children by not providing them with qualified teachers and curriculum and learning resources, they do not provide opportunities for these children to get jobs when they graduate.

In a recent study by Fuller, Wright, Gesicki, and Kang, the researchers looked at twelve diverse states by tracking test score data from 1992 until 2006. They tracked state accountability reforms from the early 1990s onward and found the positive effects of these efforts as well as evidence of narrowing achievement gaps for poor and minority students. But after 2002, as the full impact of NCLB began to take effect in public schools across the country, they found that there have been no further advances in closing the gaps and scores have since flattened out in these twelve states. They found consistent evidence that reading scores have declined since 2002, even though they had been steadily climbing under the state-led reforms of the 1990s. Since it appears that student learning as document by test scores has reached a plateau, they argue that perhaps it is time to question whether the focus on standards-based accountability is appropriate in trying to narrow the achievement gap.

The Education Trust has also documented that whatever gains promised by accountability supporters in closing the achievement gap for Hispanic and black students have not materialized. The math and reading skills of these students at the twelfth grade level are below the proficiency achieved by white children in the seventh grade. In essence, the gap has widened and not narrowed while at the same time student learning has also been hampered by Supreme Court rulings allowing for schools to resegregate.

RESEGREGATION AND STUDENT LEARNING

While school reform and accountability are forcing many teachers into practicing a pedagogy of poverty with their students—more and more of whom are "at-risk" and children of color—the issue of race has once again become central to who goes to school where, and with whom. In a trio of U.S. Supreme Court rulings in the *Dowell*, *Freeman*, and *Jenkins* cases between 1991 and 1995, schools in Oklahoma City, DeKalb County, Georgia, and Missouri reverted to the separate but unequal pattern of the Jim Crow era. Today, none of the twenty-five largest central U.S. city school systems serves a majority of white students, even though each of these locations contains a white majority population. Nearly two-thirds of the country's black children live in these cities and now attend segregated schools. These rulings have created a nearly absolute apartheid public school system in urban cities across the country where few of these children of color know any white children.

Since the 1971 *Swann* ruling enforced busing in the Charlotte-Mecklenberg (North Carolina) school system, ten million white families nationwide have moved out of cities and into suburbs or have put their children in private schools, leaving inner-city schools with large numbers of children of color. The converse exists in the suburbs, where this influx has created white segregated schools. This white flight, begun in the 1950s and 1960s has continued, thus accentuating the connection between race, income, and school location.

Gary Orfield, director of Harvard's Civil Rights Project, issued a 2001 report, *Schools More Separate*, and he states that while the country and its students are now more diverse than ever and will continue to grow more diverse, schools have remained segregated and are becoming more so. Further, these schools remain unequal because segregation by race correlates with segregation by poverty. Since a significantly large number of African American, Hispanic, and Native American children live in low-income households, the implications for resegregation of public schools should be clear: as schools grow more racially segregated, they will also re-stratify along economic lines producing more high poverty schools populated disproportionately by non-whites. This demographic shift creates significant issues for urban children. As Boger notes, student achievement is influenced greatly by the educational background and aspirations of other students in school. If schools are re-segregated, then many urban children will run the risk of being surrounded by children with challenged backgrounds and minimal aspirations, and this will have an impact on their achievement.

Collateral Damage

Differences in racial/ethnic makeup, student achievement with measurable comparable school performance, along with a teaching-to-the-test mentality have all challenged and changed the landscape of urban education. At the start of the 1990s, it appeared that state educational leaders like California's Bill Honig and New York's Tom Sobol, in collaboration with their selected experts and the business community, would dominate and direct this conversation about results and measures, rather than about content and the growing diversity of the school population. In fact, public schools are now viewed by the business community as ripe for "take-over" in much the same way that health care was privatized thirty years ago. Calling it a "highly localized industry ripe for change," Mary Tanner, the managing director of Lehman Brothers, foresees the same pattern emerging in education as did in health care. These "Educational Management Organizations" or EMOs are being touted as the answer to poor school districts with old buildings, with the emphasis on financial returns rather than on the well-being of students.

Now, in the new millennium, the federal governmental has taken firm control of both the agenda and the conversation about how to fix our schools and our children with the NCLB Act of 2001, championed by the administration of George W. Bush and his first Secretary of Education Rod Paige. In many ways, the NCLB legislation is the logical outcome of a trend put into motion by the flawed report of *A Nation at Risk*, a report championed by President Bush in 1989 and sustained and expanded upon by Bill Clinton throughout the 1990s.

But these politicians and business people have missed the point about schools and learning. What is evident to parents and educators and noted by poet and chair for the National Endowment for the Arts, Dana Goia, is that our education system has become one which produces students who can take tests and be entry-level workers rather than one which creates productive citizens for a free society. Paige and Bush have created a system that works well for businesses, however, because there is an obvious bonanza for testing and publishing companies and supplemental service providers such as Sylvan and Kaplan. These companies report that their revenue for the elementary and secondary school division has doubled since NCLB was passed.

The devastating effects of this focus on testing are apparent in most schools—particularly those in urban areas. Teaching is being narrowed to standardized and scripted lessons. Art, music, and physical education are offered in small doses, if at all; recess is eliminated and field trips are banned. Kohn notes that developmentally appropriate education and heterogeneous grouping and multiage classrooms are being abandoned as soon as test scores show no improvement according to NCLB standards. Therefore, parents and educators in urban schools need to search for ways to make their urban schools immune to this kind of tug of war which not only endangers student learning but it also can destroy the culture of the school. Several Web sites that provide clear, up-to-date information about current school reform include the following.

Internet Sources for Current School Reform

- Council for Exceptional Children: http://alquemie.smartbrief.com.
- Education Week: http://edweek.org.
- National Education Association: http://nea.org.
- Government Accounting Office: http://www.gao.gov.

UNDER ATTACK: PARENTS, EDUCATORS, COMMUNITIES, AND STATES RESPOND TO FEDERAL REFORM

Almost from the outset of its passage, NCLB has faced an increasingly vocal barrage of criticism from parents, state legislators, educators, teacher unions, and community groups on two specific points: NCLB is an unfunded federal mandate which requires huge amounts of testing. The overemphasis on testing leads to an overreliance on the test results and dictates the actions of the schools based on those results. According to Clarke, sales of printed materials related to these tests have nearly tripled to $592 million since 2002, draining funds away from public school budgets. Not surprisingly some forty-seven states are in open rebellion against the act because of this huge financial burden it places on the public school budgets in their states.

The NCLB law, as well as certain provisions under its jurisdiction, has come under attack from these various groups. Even though at least thirty state legislatures have informed Washington about their problems with NCLB, the Bush administration has been slow to amend the act in any significant way until just within the past two years. The Department of Education has, however, issued various amendments or clarifications to explain the provisions of the act in the following areas: the requirements for highly qualified teachers, the timetable for AYP, testing requirements for special needs students, waivers for state and specific cities, and changes in the time limits for non-English speaking students to become part of the school's accountability report.

Finally, a group of professors of educational communications and technology took a different direction in protesting federal interventions by created a nationwide initiative to help state departments of education facilitate the transformation of local school systems within their states. Called Future-Minds: Transforming School Systems, the initiative has a vision for schooling that will move systems away from the old way of thinking about schools as an assembly line where students are sorted to a new image better suited to personalized teaching and learning. The group seeks transformation of school systems on three levels: at the district level within the community and its stakeholders; at the district level with teachers, supervisors, and administrators; and within the district's internal culture (see www.futureminds.us).

THE CHARGE: GETTING INVOLVED IN YOUR SCHOOLS

Now that you see the historical, social, and political context of what is happening in urban schools as well as the fall-out from the NCLB legislation, we hope that you will take action within your local community and school. While your actions may not relate directly to the NCLB mandates described in this chapter, you need to be aware of them in order to navigate the political landscape of your school and school district. Further, we hope that this background will help you to understand why your school may not be making the kind of efforts you would hope for to build authentic partnerships with parents and community members. It may very well be that they are so preoccupied with dealing with the legislative mandates that they have not been able to devote adequate time to forming authentic partnerships in the community. In the next chapter you will see the conditions you need in order to form effective partnerships. You will also see examples of effective partnerships in urban schools and school districts. In the final chapter you will see ways to act within your own community. Obviously in the midst of the current political climate and atmosphere of distrust of schools and teachers, your efforts are desperately needed. We hope these images, concepts, strategies, and examples can help you in your efforts.

NOTE

Portions of this chapter were published in expanded form as Chapter 9 in Marshall, J. Dan, et al. *Turning Points in Curriculum: A Contemporary American Memoir*, 2nd ed. Published by Allyn and Bacon, Boston, MA. Copyright © 2007 by Pearson Education. Adapted by permission of the publisher.

REFERENCES

Bracey, G. W. (2007). Things fall apart: NCLB self-destructs. *Phi Delta Kappan*, 88(6), 475–476.

Carnegie Foundation. (1988). *An Imperiled Generation: Saving Urban Schools*. Princeton, NJ: Princeton University Press.

Censored 2003. (2003). "Corporations promote HMO model for school districts," Project Censored, eds. New York: Seven Stories Press.

Cremin, L. (1990). *Popular Education and Its Discontents*. New York: Harper & Row.

Darling-Hammond, L. (2007). The flat earth and education: How America's commitment to equity will determine our future. *Educational Researcher*, (36), 6, 318–334.

Fuller, B., Wright, J., Geisicki, K., and Kang, E. (2007). Gauging growth: How to judge *No Child Left Behind*. *Educational Researcher*, 6(36), 268–278.

Gibboney, R. A. (2006). Centennial reflections: Intelligence through design. *Phi Delta Kappan*, 88 (2), 170–172.

Haberman, M. (1991). The pedagogy of poverty versus good teaching. *Phi Delta Kappan*, 73(4), 290–294.

Hursh, D. (2007). Exacerbating inequality: The failed promise of the No Child Left Behind Act. *Race Ethnicity and Education*, 10(3), 295–308.

Kohn, A. (2004) Test today, privatize tomorrow: Using accountability to "reform" public schools to death. *Phi Delta Kappan*, 85(8), 568–77.

Kozol, J. (2005). *The Shame of the Nation: The Restoration of Apartheid Schooling in America*. New York: Crown Publishers.

National Education Association. (2005). "NCLB results offer complex and muddled picture."

Orfield, G., ed. (2004). *Drop-Outs in America: Confronting the Graduation Rate Crisis*. Cambridge, MA: Harvard Education Press.

Popham, J. (1999). Why standardized tests don't measure educational quality. *Educational Leadership*, (56), 6, 8–15.

Rury, J. (2005). Introduction: The changing social contours of urban education. In J. Rury, (Ed.), *Urban Education in the United States: A Historical Reader* (pp. 1–12). New York: Palgrave Macmillan.

Songer, N. B., Lee, H. S., and Kam, R. (2002). Technology-rich inquiry in urban classrooms: What are the barriers to inquiry pedagogy? *Journal of Research in Science Teaching*, 39(2), 128–150.

Swanson, C. B. (2008). *Cities in Crisis: A Special Analytical Report on High School Graduation*. Bethesda, MD: Editorial Projects in Education Research Center.

CHAPTER 7

Building Blocks for Reform Coalitions: Continuing the Conversation

The research in recent years is quite clear: parent involvement makes a significant difference in schools. When parents get involved, children achieve more in schools and, as a result, earn higher grades. In addition, children attend school more, exhibit more positive behaviors while they are there, and are more likely to stay in school. Children whose parents get involved are also less likely to be retained or placed in special education. When parents get involved, students' motivation increases, they become more engaged in their own learning and they see themselves as competent and capable. In addition, they learn to regulate their own behavior and leaning by setting goals for themselves. Further, when parents and community members get involved by supporting a specific subject matter (i.e. math), children make significant gains in that subject matter. Research also indicates that students are not the only ones who benefit from their parents' involvement in schools. Parents reap benefits as well. By getting involved, they better understand the school's curriculum, programs, and activities. Teachers also benefit because they increase their awareness of family perspectives and recognize threats to stereotyping that could compromise relationships as well as how they work with their students.

Some urban schools and school districts are focusing on increased parent involvement as a significant reform initiative. Some formal programs to promote parent involvement include James Comer's School Development Program and the Industrial Areas Foundation (IAF)—a multiethnic, interfaith organization that focuses on urban neighborhoods of the working poor. Some of these projects also get the community involved including churches, civic groups, and other agencies. Not all schools are involved in these initiatives, and those that are working to increase parent involvement are often trying to juggle this initiative with a number of others. With this in mind we believe it is critical that parents realize they cannot sit back and assume the schools will take the lead in getting them and their community involved. It is ultimately up to the parents to initiate the kinds of relationships they want and need within their schools.

WHY IS IT SO HARD TO MAINTAIN AUTHENTIC RELATIONSHIPS WITH YOUR SCHOOLS?

The culture of an urban school is not always conducive to creating sustained and meaningful relationships between the school, parents, and community. Even though a number of urban schools are located within specific urban communities, they are often not seen as part of the community. Teachers and administrators are rarely members of the community itself. Instead they come in from other, often more affluent, areas of the city or from the suburbs. They often drive to school in a bubble, park in a gated lot, and enter and exit the school building without any contact with families or businesses that surround the school. When teachers and school leaders have no contact with the actual community, they run the risk of not understanding the community and its members. As a result, they risk maintaining a deficit mind-set for the students and their families.

Further, when the schools attempt to partner with universities, agencies, and businesses, they often form these partnerships with entities outside of the immediate community. Thus, even those outside stakeholders who are involved in making decisions for the school are often not members of that immediate community. Historical precedent also comes into play in the culture of urban schools. Particularly in the 1970s and 1980s, many urban students were bused to schools outside of their local community to try to manage the desegregation of schools. It has only been in the recent decade that school districts have made greater efforts to send students to their community schools in hopes to get the parents and community more involved.

Another reason why it is difficult for parents and community members to form relationships with schools is based on how parents and community members often view their roles in working with schools—with individualist versus collective efforts. When you hear politicians talk about urban schools, you often hear them talk about the potential for individuals to improve their lives based on their education. Everyone has the opportunity to succeed academically, and academic success leads to success in life. There are two big problems with this line of reasoning. First, it is wrong. Research indicates that students who live in oppressed urban areas do not have a level playing field when it comes to employment. Even for those students who graduate from high school, employers often pass them by because they attended urban high schools that have bad reputations. Employers often assume that the education they received at the urban school was substandard, so whatever achievements the students may make while attending the urban school are discounted. Second, the focus on the individual in urban schools comes at the cost of the community itself. In urban areas, particularly poor urban areas, you cannot separate the conditions within the schools from the conditions within the community. Individuals within these communities rarely gain power individually—they gain power as a community when they focus on the community.

Parents often see their involvement in schools in terms of helping their children with homework at night. Other parents may envision helping out by volunteering in classrooms. These examples of involvement may be what the parents experienced when they were students and their parents were involved in schools. While this work is important and, as research indicates, can lead to increased levels of student achievement, we feel it is also important that parents and community members get involved in the larger school community. When parents get involved in the larger context of the school and the school community, more meaningful relationships can be formed between stakeholders. Further, when parents get involved at the level of school operations, they are more likely to continue their involvement as their students move to middle and high school—times when parent involvement often declines drastically. Parents who are involved at the school and/or community level often move beyond whatever images they have of schools from their own experience as students to see current challenges and opportunities in today's urban schools. Thus, as a parent or community member, we challenge you to provide alternative images for other parents and community members so they can see meaningful ways they can help that move beyond homework and serving within the individual classrooms alone. Instead, they can see ways their enlarged images of involvement in schools can focus on the school and its community.

HOW DO PARENTS GET INVOLVED?

Two researchers, Hoover-Dempsey and Sandler, developed a framework that explores how and why parents get involved in schools. We think it is important for parents who want to get others involved to see why parents may get involved. It is important to recognize that not everyone has the same motivation or the same level of confidence to get involved in their child's school and community. Hoover-Dempsey and Sandler identified five levels of how parents get involved that will help you recognize the potential opportunities and challenges you may face in trying to get others involved. It will also help you and whatever parent association you may support to make the best use of parents and community members as resources. Based on these levels, we offer potential applications for you as you try to increase the level of involvement.

The first level of parental involvement provides three motivations for why parents initially choose to get involved: how parents see themselves as parents, the degree to which they feel they are capable of helping in school, and the opportunities that are readily available to get involved. In order for parents to get involved at this initial level, they have to see themselves as good parents who are capable of doing something good for the school. Further, they need obvious opportunities through which they can get involved. With this in mind, it is good to have fairly easy opportunities that will get parents into the building with fairly easy tasks to help reinforce the parent's initial thoughts that they can be helpful. What can parent associations do to support more parents and get them to choose to get involved in schools? The first and most critical step is for parents, teachers, and administrators alike to avoid jumping to conclusions when they see parents who are not involved. Parents may not get involved because they lack the confidence to make any sort of significant contribution. If parents had negative experiences in schools or if they struggle with language barriers, they will be less likely to get involved. The parents may feel that they do not have the necessary skills to help out. If these parents see most of the work being doing by more affluent and more educated parents, their insecurities and doubts may be reinforced. Involved parents need to be sensitive to these issues and find ways to encourage parent involvement without appearing to be condescending to these parents or otherwise operating with some sort of deficit mind-set—reserving easier or menial efforts for those parents who are less educated or who lack financial resources. Instead, involved parents and parent organizations need to recognize what all parents have to offer to the school community as equal and vital contributions.

While the first level of the Hoover-Dempsey and Sandler model for parent involvement in the framework determines whether parents will get involved, the second level determines how they will get involved and stay involved because it deals with parents' specific knowledge and skills as well as how much time they have to give based upon other commitments at work and home. This second level also addresses the specific requests from students and teachers that have a significant impact on how and how much parents get involved. According to Hoover-Dempsey and Sandler, parents will get involved when they are asked to do something with clearly defined parameters and if their jobs or other family commitments do not prevent them from doing it. With this in mind, how can a parent association influence the rate of parent involvement? One way would be to help teachers identify specific ways parents could help in classrooms and in the school in general and then help the teachers to write up clear "job descriptions" for the volunteer opportunities. The parent association could also help teachers who may otherwise be reluctant to seek parent involvement—particularly in instances where there are cultural or language differences that may contribute to the teachers' lack of soliciting parent help. Parent associations can also identify creative ways to let parents get involved when it is more convenient for their schedules. Letting parents volunteer to support the school in the evenings or on the weekends may be one way to do this. In addition, the school or school community could use specific holidays such as Labor Day or Martin Luther King Jr. Day as a time to support the school through community service. For the parents who have busy and otherwise unusual schedules, parent associations may also find ways they can provide virtual support for schools and teachers. For example, parents who are technologically savvy could use their skills to find appropriate Web sites to support the school curriculum. Parents could also help identify grant opportunities and work on writing the grants electronically. We will discuss means through which this sort of help may be possible later in this chapter.

At the third level of the Hoover-Dempsey and Sandler model, parents' efforts in the schools have a direct impact on students. At this level parents move beyond the more generalized notions of helping out in schools to see that their efforts actually make a difference not only in the school itself but also in the lives of the children in the school. It becomes more than just painting a mural on the cafeteria wall that makes the school look good. Their efforts may influence the achievement of students other than their own, or it may help a group of refugees who have come to the school to feel more welcomed and prepared. At this level you have even greater potential for building meaningful relationships and a sense of community. Parents move beyond doing something for the building or something for the student population in general and begin to influence the lives of those who are part of the community. Parent associations can achieve this level of involvement with parents if they are able to identify authentic ways parents can get involved and make a difference, share with parents how their efforts will make a difference, and then measure those differences as parents get involved to validate the work and encourage future involvement. For example, a parent association may design a program where parents tutor children in reading. They may solicit the help of a nearby university to teach the parents how to teach literacy skills. When seeking volunteers, the association could convey the importance of this program to parents by focusing on the need to increase literacy within the school. Once the program is in place, parents could keep track of how well students do who have participated in the program and then share that information with the volunteers as well as with future potential volunteers. Creating ways for parents and community members to get involved and directly influence student outcomes ultimately supports meaningful relationships among all stakeholders—teachers and administrators see other stakeholders as taking on responsibility for desired outcomes within the school. This could also help prevent or at least minimize the situation where varied stakeholders operate from an us-them dichotomy—one where teachers are there to teach and parents are there to stay busy with things that have nothing to do with teaching. Instead, it helps all stakeholders to stay focused on the mission and vision of the school and for all stakeholders to see that their participation makes a difference.

At the fourth level in the Hoover-Dempsey and Sandler model, parents begin to work more independently because they have developed skills and capacity and have a more sophisticated understanding of appropriate support. So, for example, parents who may have tutored from a fairly prescriptive model or who may have supported instruction by administering prescriptive reading inventories may begin to recognize ways students are struggling with their reading and, as a result, can use specific strategies to help them. Further, the school and volunteers, because their work is getting more and more embedded, negotiate their expectations with the parents' involvement so that there is a good fit. If you hope to get parents involved at this level, you will need to build and sustain significant infrastructure to enhance the capacity of parents to support teachers and administrators in meaningful ways. To do this, you will have to not only think about the programs designed to help the students and the school, you will also need to think about, develop, and sustain programs to support parents as they support the school. This level of involvement will require resources for training and support as well.

While this level of commitment will, in and of itself, help to build relationships between teachers, leaders, and parents, it also requires stronger ties in order to be successful, so stakeholders will need additional opportunities to learn from one another in order for the partnership to be effective. It will also require parents to develop meaningful relationships with other parents—mentoring and modeling the skills and practices that support the school to help involve more parents. Without ensuring a way to add to the number of parents involved at this level, your group of parents runs the risk of forming an elite and exclusive team of volunteers who have a higher status in the partnership based upon the skills and knowledge they have acquired. While a "super team" of instructional support may seem efficient, ultimately an exclusive group of parent volunteers may have a negative effect on the overall community if that group appears elite.

In addition to the need to train, support, and mentor future parent volunteers, you will need to work with teachers and administrators to foster a climate of trust. When teachers and administrators open up the school for parents to get involved in practices that reflect the core values and goals of the school, they must trust that parents will not fail them. This can be a challenge when, as we have mentioned, the teachers and administrators may not have had close ties with parents and community members in the past. They may find that parents see the work and the aims of the school differently than they do, and this may cause tensions as they begin to work together. To illustrate, consider the first few months of living with a new partner or spouse—no matter how much you may have known about that person prior to living with one another, you may or may not have been prepared for the challenges you face living with one another. It takes time to learn to compromise and accept things about one another that may be different from what you expected or different from the way you live and work. The same can be said when partners come together in a school and begin to work together. Each partner has to learn about the ways the other works and trust that even if that work is different, the partner is making a meaningful contribution.

At the final level of the model, stakeholders experience coherence with their efforts and the mission of the school. They see that they are making a difference in the lives of children in the school and that they are actually contributing to the overall school mission. They begin to see how their efforts, however small, actually influence the mission of the school and help the school achieve its larger goals. When stakeholders achieve this level, they are able to create a sustainable space for change within schools. Their efforts will be responsive to whatever changes may come regarding the goals and mission of the school because they will be predisposed to think on this larger scale regarding their efforts. Even if the leadership in the school changes, stakeholders should be able to maintain their relationships with one another and they should be able to continue their work without interruption. For a parent association to influence this level of involvement, parents need to be involved in the very core planning and purpose-building process within the school. This requires a significant level of trust among all stakeholders, and that requires a significant amount of time to develop and nurture. To the greater the degree that your parent association becomes a critical part of the school's operations, then the more likely you will be able to work toward this level of involvement.

Hoover-Demsey and Sandler Model for Parent Involvement

- Will parents get involved?

- How will parents get involved?

- How will parents' efforts influence student outcomes?

- How will parents' efforts become a natural part of the school's efforts?

- How will parents' work become a vital part of the school's goals and mission?

WHAT WOULD AUTHENTIC PARTICIPATION LOOK LIKE?

While the model from Hoover-Dempsey and Sander offers ways to view parents' commitment to get involved and its effects, we still need to look at the interactions within the school and identify authentic participation. Anderson offers five qualities of authentic participation that we believe apply to collaboration between parents, community members, and the school: broad inclusion, relevant participation, authentic local conditions and processes, coherence between means and ends of participation, and focus on broader structural inequalities. We encourage you to explore each of these qualities based upon the relationships you have with your community school. First, who is involved in work with the schools? Do the parents who are currently involved—whatever that capacity may be—represent the diversity of the community itself? Are mothers and fathers involved? Grandparents? Individuals who do not yet have children in the schools? Community members who do not have children in the schools? If groups of people within your community are not represented in the work of the school, then you lose their insights and perspectives within that work. This becomes particularly problematic when schools and their communities offer the appearance of meaningful and authentic participation, but when you look closely at the makeup of the advisory committees, P.T.A.'s, and other collaborative efforts, you see trends in who is present—and more importantly, who is absent from the decision-making process.

Second, what kind of work are parents and community members doing with schools? Is that work meaningful? Consider the following scenario. In the early to mid-nineties there was a prominent movement in schools across the United States referred to as "site-based management," where teachers became more involved in the decision-making process. At the time, one of the authors visited a number of schools that claimed to be site-based management schools. In a number of cases, teachers were involved in decision making, but the decisions they were making were relatively meaningless. One site-base team of teachers, for example, spent more than an hour debating the time that the students should be able to go out on the playground and sign each other's year books. Another team debated the merits of assigned parking for teachers. Yet another group spent several meetings arguing about the reassignment of classrooms for the upcoming year. In each of these instances, teachers took on more responsibility and were "empowered" to make decisions about their schools. However, these issues were peripheral to the real work they needed to do, and, in fact, often distracted them from tackling the real issues about curriculum, instruction, professional support, etc. Parents and community members may also be distracted by relatively minor and inconsequential issues within schools. Often this takes the form of fund raising or special events planned for families and/or teachers. When these issues take on such importance that they consume the collaborative energy of stakeholders, then they are actually destructive forces in any kind of collaborative work.

Third, to what degree does your participation with the school fit with your other work as a member of your community? To what degree does your community support collaborative efforts outside of the school and thus reinforce collaboration with the school? To what degree, if any, have community organizations or associations collaborated with schools in the past? Often, community organizations avoid working with and for schools because they are so complex. When communities do get involved in schools, they often do so in the form of full-service schools where support services in health and social work are brought into the school building. Some also form local school councils to help in decision making. Both of these examples fall short of authentic participation. Councils can exist and services can be provided without any real relationships being formed. While these community influences may share in space and possibly decision-making power, they do not necessarily share in values. At best, this then becomes a technical partnership void of any real shared vision for the school and the community together. Furthermore, if an urban community is rife with bureaucracy and political turmoil, then very little progress will be made when you try to work with your local school. You want to decrease any possible barriers to your work with schools—including the context of the broader community. If you do not first try to minimize barriers to your work in schools, then you will waste a significant amount of energy reacting to those problems along the way. You also need to be aware of how your community functions as a community. How do people come together and network? What are the dynamics of economically powerful businesses in the area as well as local politicians? What other collaborative efforts within your community succeeded? What other partnerships failed? What can you learn about your community from these examples?

Fourth, what do you hope to gain by virtue of your work with the schools? What are your ultimate aims for the collaboration? Do the means through which you work to achieve those aims match up with those aims? It is very easy to fall into doing what works at the expense of what is right. For example, a school may want to increase family literacy within a local community. To achieve this, they may open up the school at various times in the evening and on the weekend to allow families to come and preview books for sale at a book fair. The school may focus largely on advertising and provide incentives for participation. This effort may create tensions because a number of the families in the area do not have the financial resources needed to purchase books. Thus, rather than increase the likelihood that families will read together, the school community may inadvertently reinforce the social class distinctions of the neighborhood. Particularly in the many gentrifying neighborhoods of cities, these social class distinctions may fall along ethnic and racial lines—thus creating even more tensions in the kinds of relationships students and their school community seek to maintain. Even if your sense of purpose is not misguided as in the previous example, focusing on individualistic purposes, as we have mentioned above, can become problematic. For many, education is about individual achievement. Rarely if ever do you hear someone argue that schools should support thoughtful citizenship in order to create and sustain democratic communities. Without some larger purpose, collaboration will be difficult, if not impossible, to sustain.

Finally, any sort of authentic participation between you and your school will require you to examine broader structural inequalities inherent within your community and within the school district itself. In most if not all urban districts, you are very likely to see that not all schools are created equally. For example, examine the lunch menu of a number of schools within your district for a week or two. You will, in all likelihood, notice that schools in affluent areas may offer more variety and better quality food than those in poorer areas where a higher percentage of the school's students need the assistance of a free or reduced price for lunch. Along those same lines, note how those who get assistance through free and reduced lunches or through other means are tagged or distinguished from others. Do students going through the line at lunch have a different colored lunch card than those who are not supported by free or reduced lunch? When the book fair comes to the school, do these students get special colored coupons to use to get a free book while those with the financial means bring their cash? What happens to the students who cannot bring in money for field trips? These concerns are not just found within the school. Is your local public library easily accessible by public transportation? Are families with limited transportation forced to purchase most of their groceries from a substandard grocery store that charges higher prices? Do city workers attend to potholes and other safety concerns in affluent/gentrified parts of your community more quickly than in other areas? You may not notice these inequities unless you are looking at your community with a critical perspective. While it may not be easy or natural, it is nevertheless critical that you explore how power and wealth (or the lack of both) influence your community. If you see clear examples of inequality in your community, then you need to first address these inequalities before you begin your work with the schools.

So, based on what we have discussed so far in this chapter, you know that participation within urban schools is a challenge. You know parents come to participate in schools with very different motivations and levels of apprehension. You also know participation takes a tremendous amount of work in order to be truly authentic. If you do not take the time to explore these five questions, then your efforts will be in vain or possibly even damaging to the overall culture of the school community. We urge you to take some time to review failures in your school and community—learn why they failed. While history never really repeats itself exactly, you may be able to discern trends based upon things that have happened in the past. In reviewing both successes and failures, try to move away from specific players (unless, of course, they are still key players in the school or community) and explore the dynamics of the situations. You may also gain a great deal by learning about other community efforts within your city. Are there other parent and/or community associations that succeeded or failed when they sought change? If so, identify key stakeholders in those initiatives (both the successes and the failures) and take them out for coffee to learn from them. Again, you will not be able to merely replicate what they have done, but you can learn factors that may contribute to success and failure in your own efforts.

Five Questions to Determine Your Potential for Authentic Participation

✎ Who is involved with the work in your school?

✎ What kind of work are parents and community members doing in the schools?

✎ To what degree does your participation with the school fit with your other work as a member of your community?

✎ What do you hope to gain by virtue of your work with the schools?

✎ What broad structural inequalities exist within your school community, and how can you overcome these inequalities?

MAKING SCHOOL AND COMMUNITY A SHARED SPACE

We cannot emphasize enough that parents and community members need to take the initiative to help form authentic relationships with and for schools and their communities. You cannot afford to sit back and wait for the schools to initiate these relationships. Schools, as we noted in Chapter 6, are under an extreme amount of pressure based upon the No Child Left Behind (NCLB) legislation, and as such they often do not have the time of flexibility to initiate extended and extensive relationships with parents and community members. Further, teachers and leaders often do not have the political leverage to make extensive partnerships happen. Without being able to show its direct relationships with increased test scores and because authentic partnerships are not part of a specific reform model, many urban schools would struggle with attempts to justify allocation of resources to developing and nurturing partnerships with parents and communities.

Parents and community members who organize and develop skills to navigate the official and political operations of a school district will have far more power than the teachers or school leaders. These parents and community members can make demands of the district without fear of professional reprisal. In essence, you have no jobs within the district to lose. Further, when parents organize the shared collaborative space of a school and its community, that space is not as regulated as it would be if it was formed and controlled by the school or school district. For example, some parent associations acquire nonprofit status and function outside of a school's P.T.A. so they can offer fund raisers for the school that involve alcohol. They are able to raise more money for the school based upon fewer restrictions on how they raise that money.

Some of you may feel uncomfortable with the ambiguous charge to go and form meaningful relationships with your schools. It may be difficult to envision what these relationships might look like. While we do not want to give you a recipe to follow, we will offer images of what authentic partnerships may look like. For starters, we offer three examples of collaborative spaces that can be created and sustained by parents: a parent center, a study circle, and a parent association. Keep in mind that these are merely examples of how, as parents, you can get involved in your child's school. We strongly encourage you to go beyond the three examples given here and explore other ways parents have created structures within which they support their schools and their communities.

Parent Centers

Parent centers can serve a variety of functions. A parent center is a governance model for schools that provides the structure created and sustained by parents to allow parents to get involved in the operation of the school. Often these centers are supported through the use of Title I or other supplemental funds. When this model is interactive, parents plan for and design this space within the school. It is essential to get other parents involved in the center, and the best way to do that is to visit parents at their homes to discuss the school parent center, its purpose, and its function. Parents also have the authority to set priorities for the center, and researchers recommend that parents actually staff the center including the position of center coordinator. Once a center is established, the staff at the center needs to get as many people in the community involved as possible. This often takes creative programs and incentives to get otherwise busy parents to come to the school and help. For example, a center in Boston offers breakfasts for fathers, grandfathers, and uncles to come and learn about the opportunities to serve within the center. Another center offers small gifts to teenage mothers who come to parenting classes.

A parent center should also find meaningful ways to demonstrate that the children are the focus of their efforts. Some centers showcase student work. Others offer award ceremonies. In another, students come to the center after school for tutoring by parent volunteers. The parent center is also a place where parents come to interact with the school staffs and build relationships with them. In one center, parents and teachers come together and develop and sign learning contracts for their students. By having the contracts signed at the center, it takes the difference in power away from the situation that often exists when it is done in the teacher's classroom.

Parent centers are designed to take over much of the interaction between the school and the parents. As such, they need to have sufficient resources to make the relationships more meaningful. The centers also distribute much of the formal information exchanged between parents and the school. Again, a parent center is a space where neither group is "in control," so the focus can be on the issues at hand rather than the position and power of the school or the parents. As such, the parent center can be a source of positive messages sent between the home and the school, whereas in many schools the limited contact parents and schools have is often related to problems the student is having.

Finally, the parent center should be accessible when parents can come to it. For this reason, it is critical that the center is staffed by parents and community members and not just operated by teachers and other school personnel on top of everything else they do. Making connections when it is possible and convenient for parents and others to attend often means teachers are expected to attend a large number of functions in the evenings. While it is important that teachers are available for some evening functions, schools should not expect them to spend a large number of evenings away from their own families—particularly when those teachers are often bringing work home with them and possibly attending graduate school on top of their already busy schedules. Not only should the center be accessible at convenient hours, it should also be welcoming for parents. Parents within the school community should feel comfortable coming to the center regardless of their own educational background. With this in mind, the décor of the center should be inviting, and staff should consider maintaining, however simple, snacks and coffee for parents and school staff to come together informally and talk.

One such parent center is the Amherst Regional High School Parent Center. This center is located in Amherst, Massachusetts, and it states the following as its mission:

> The mission of the Amherst Regional High School Parent Center is to enhance communication and involvement among parents/guardians of all backgrounds and origins, the school, and the community, to promote the well being of all ARHS students, and reflect the racial, ethnic, and social-economic diversity of the student body.

The center sends out newsletters seven times a year to keep stakeholders informed. It also supports a number of initiatives. One such resource is informational meetings for parents. For example, the center hosted a meeting where someone from the district attorney's office came and discussed Internet safety. The center also hosts study circles where parents, students, and teachers address issues of equity and excellence in the school. Further, it allocates 10 percent of its budget for small grants for teachers, students, staff, and parents who want to do something for the school. The center offers support ranging from $50 to $100 with these small grants. It also supports a group identified as RaDAR. This group focuses on race, discipline, action, and rights. This group works to end racism, prejudice, and discrimination from policies, practices, attitudes, and procedures within the school. As a result of this group, the school has made changes within its student handbook as well as its selection processes for honor roll and cheerleading and its disciplinary practices.

Study Circles

Study circles are a second structure through which parents can get involved. Study circles are groups of typically eight to twelve individuals who come together two hours a week for four to six weeks to explore an issue regarding the school. When forming study circles, it is important to seek participants who come with diverse experiences and perspective. It is also important to develop democratic ways of functioning within the group. Facilitators of the groups can be trained at the Study Circles Resource Center. If this training is not available, then facilitators should have sufficient interpersonal skills to engage the group and to help resolve conflicts should they arise. The facilitators should also be or become familiar with action research and how it is implemented within schools. This support may be available at a partnering university in the area.

In Rockville, Maryland, the school district has set up study circles in a number of their schools. Each circle involves fifteen people, including parents, teachers, and students, who meet for six two-hour sessions. Each circle is guided by two trained facilitators. The circles have dealt with issues such as race and equity, English as a second language, and student achievement. The study circles take what they learn during their sessions and then translate that information into action. These actions have included increasing bilingual teachers where needed, dealing with issues of equity, and increasing a school's capacity for more study circles.

Local Parent Associations

The third structure through which parents can get involved are through local parent associations. Local parent associations are formed independent of the school and operate from their own funding and governance structure. Some parent associations are informal and require only limited financial support. Others develop a more formal governance structure and acquire significant financial resources that they use to support the school. Some parent associations achieve tax-exempt status to increase their fund-raising potential. Parent associations have the potential to make clear and mean-ingful connections between the school and its community because both the school and the community can see the benefits of the mutual support. We will provide a specific example of a parent association later in this chapter. Like the parent centers that function outside of the school, parent associa-tions can also provide a space where teachers, administrators, parents, and community members can come together as equals and make decisions about a school and its community.

VIRTUAL SPACES FOR PARENT INVOLVEMENT

Technology is a powerful force within our society, and a number of par-ents have started to use the Internet as a way to network and find support for their children. There are a number of sites where parents rate their children's schools, and its teachers. There are chat lines where parents can discuss spe-cific concerns, find out about resources, and learn about new initiatives in schools and districts. Given the powerful influence of technology today, par-ents can explore ways to harness the Internet and other technological means to create spaces through which families can be involved in school commu-nity. We make this suggestion with one warning—parents need to make sure they are not denying access to certain populations within the school by virtue of using technology. If your school has a wide range of socioeconomic levels among families, then using technology will, in all likelihood, give the more affluent families advantages over those who may not have access to the Internet at home. In such a case, we encourage you to pursue grant funds to get computers and Internet access for parents who cannot afford it so they can be equally involved in the school–community collaboration. In addition, assess the degree to which there may be resources within the community that may be used to help parents get involved through an online environment.

Once you have secured access to all stakeholders, then you can focus on creating an authentic online environment for your work. You need to make sure it easy to operate because some parents will not have a sophisticated technological literacy. One such space online that is conducive to collaborate work is Wikispaces. Wikispaces are powerful online spaces that can be ac-cessed at www.wikispaces.com. A specific space for parent involvement can be created as a Wikispace, and parents and community members can use the space to access information, discuss issues, and plan for events. Wikispaces are ideal for parent and community collaboration because they are free and accessible to everyone. Further, all participants have equal power to influ-ence the space in terms of creating pages, etc. If the site creators want to grant access to the entire community, but they also want to limit who can make changes, they can set up the site to accommodate these restrictions. If a parent association needs to address more sensitive issues and wants to limit who can see what is happening on the site, then they can pay a small fee to restrict access to the site for only those who are invited to join. The site offers a very user-friendly way to hold a variety of discussions, and unlike some online formats, the discussions are fairly easy to follow. The following sites provide clever tutorials for navigating and creating Wikispaces: www.wikispaces.com/site/tour#introduction, www.youtube.com/watch?v=-dnL00TdmLY and www.wikispaces.com/help+teachers.

AVONDALE EDUCATION ASSOCIATION: PARENTS MAKING A DIFFERENCE

Avondale Estates is a small city located east of Atlanta. While it is not officially part of the city, it is an urban area "inside the perimeter"—a designation including it in the urban districts of Atlanta verses the many suburban districts stretching out thirty to forty miles from the center of the city. Avondale Estates is part of the DeKalb County School System—a large district spanning a broad geography and a wide range of communities in the Atlanta area. Avondale Estates has maintained a number of ways its members stay connected to one another—a community pool, a park, and a number of restaurants that local families frequent. Nevertheless, like many other gentrified areas of the city, middle and upper middle class families living there have historically sent their children to the private schools in the area. Therefore, while children saw each other at the pool and the park, they typically have not gone to school with one another.

Jill Joyner-Bush, a parent in the Avondale Estates community, wanted to change this. Four years ago, while sitting at the wade pool with her then infant son, she watched the older children playing at the pool and asked another parent where all the children went to school. When the parent began to list the various private schools in the area, Jill realized that the children in her community—and in all likelihood her own child—did not have a strong community school where they could attend together. The community's children would come together in the summer to play at the pool, and then all go their separate ways during the school year. Jill wanted to change this. She learned that another woman in the community, Sandra Ellick, was also interested in supporting the local school even though she did not yet have children. These two women got together and began to form the Avondale Education Association (AEA).

Jill and Sandra discovered that previous attempts to form a parent group for the schools often failed. In those cases the parents interested in organizing already had children in school, and they were unable to sustain an effort to influence the local school while their children attended local private schools. In contrast, Jill and Sandra were both parents of infants. They knew they had three or four years to organize and begin working with the local school before the many parents of infants and toddlers in the area would be considering where their children would attend. They began talking with parents in the area, and they used the Avondale Parent Association—a strong group already organized in the community—to inform parents about the new organization that would support the local school.

The women formed a steering committee to explore the potential of a neighborhood school and the group started holding monthly meetings. They spent the first year discussing the various options to create a local school for their children—including both public and private and public school options. They discussed two potential routes for working with the public school system: supporting the public school down the street or starting up a charter school. After a year of research and discussion, the parent association took a vote, and decided they would work with the existing public school in their neighborhood. When discussing the process, Jill noted that they felt like pioneers going through the process. She noted that for at least the past ten years parents in the area had not sent their children to the local public elementary school—so their commitment to the local school was a significant shift in what the community had done in the past.

The AEA began working with the school and immediately noticed a number of needs within it. They were discouraged by what they saw as a lack of financial support from the state and the school's district. They were also discouraged by the physical conditions within the school building, so they began raising funds and also began working with teachers to write grants for the school. The grant writing gave the group an opportunity to develop relationships with the teachers. They felt this was a critical first step because the principals often change every three to four years but the teaching staff within the school was fairly consistent.

In the past four years, the AEA has been very busy. Jill completed the paperwork to make the association a nonprofit organization. This has increased their potential for fund raising because donations are now tax deductible. In addition, the organization is able to support successful fund-raising activities in the area such as cookouts and wine tasting events because they are not restricted like the school's P.T.A. would be. Based on their fundraisers, the association has been able to donate $8,000 to the elementary school in the past two years. The association has also been involved in improving the school itself. They have held monthly campus cleanups, worked on the landscaping by having trees trimmed and planting flowers. They also step in when the school calls them with specific needs. For example, the principal called and told the organization that refugees from Ethiopia and other parts of Africa (a large percentage of the students in the school) were not able to purchase school uniforms. The parents in the association visited the various thrift stores to find uniforms for the children. The organization has also worked with parents in the community to try to get them to commit to sending their children to the school in the future. As of 2006, the association has twenty families committed to send their children to the school the following year.

At this point, the group has been more successful getting financial support and community involvement from the families in the area. They have been less successful getting parents of the infants and toddlers into the schools to volunteer.

Jill has also written an application to shift the school to charter-school status. When the association voted to support the local school, they also agreed that charter-school status within the school would give them more opportunities to be involved in the actual operations of the school. In the process of writing the charter, the association polled the teachers to determine the potential reform models and themes they would prefer to use. They also got the support of the former and new principals to convert to a charter. The group has largely explored International Baccalaureate model and themes such as a museum school or an eco-environmental school. The progress in this initiative, however, has been delayed because the state has implemented a new policy allowing districts to apply for charter-wide status, and this has put school-level charter applications on hold.

The creative solutions of the AEA seem to have led to more creative solutions among the school administrators. Whether it is because of the efforts of the AEA or not, the new principal has worked to find creative means of solving some of the school's problems. For example, she has hired an interpreter to work with the large population of Bantu families in the school. While many of the Bantu women did not work outside the home, they were not comfortable coming into the school and getting involved because of the language barriers. Now with the support of the interpreter, they are starting to come to the school to help with sewing and other tasks that do not require them to know a great deal of English. Jill added that she feels that it has been good for the children to see their mothers in the school.

At this point the AEA has about 125 families involved in the local school. The group holds potluck dinners to provide opportunities for families in the community to get to know one another and to learn about the school. As the community grows in the number of new births, the association grows as well. The association has a Web site, and they provide real estate agents with brochures about the school and the parent association. When families move into the area, a member of the association contacts them and tells them about the association. They do not pressure families to join, but they make sure the family knows about them and learns about the various opportunities to get involved.

The association has also worked with the school to improve the image of the school within the community. When people see the school's report card and the test scores published in the local paper, the school looks bad. The test scores are very low. If parents moving into the area or considering the area solely rely on the overall school report card and the scores reported in the local paper, then they have a very negative image of what is going on in the school. In response, the association works with the principal to pull out the test scores from the students in the school who have stayed since kindergarten or first grade. The scores of the students who have been in the school over time have demonstrated significantly higher scores than the transient refugee children within the school. The association offers this data to parents that move in the area.

What can we learn from the AEA? The parent organization's success is not haphazard. They deliberately developed a dynamic and influential force within the local community. A number of factors have influenced the degree to which the association has been successful: time, education/training, securing support, negotiating multiple needs within the school and community, investing in structure and capacity of the association, public relations, and becoming an indispensable element within the community and the school.

Jill, Sandra, and all of the parents involved from the beginning of the association have always realized that real change takes time. For Jill, the time to get involved was when her first child was an infant. For Sandra, the time to get involved was before she even had children. Most of the parents involved in the association will not "need" the public school for three to four years. They recognize that they need to invest in the community school early in order to see some of the changes take form by the time their children attend.

The association has also been successful because its members have invested energy and resources in education and training. For example, Jill's background is in fund-raising, but she did not merely rely on her past work and volunteer experience. She took advantage of leadership training offered within the area to be better prepared to support the association. In addition, one of the first priorities of the association was to educate the families in the area about schooling and about the community school. The group spent a year educating everyone about the possible options for the local school.

The association has also worked hard to secure support from the many stakeholders in the school. They initially sought the support of the teachers because they knew the teachers were a more stable factor in the school than the administration. As the administration shifted, the association worked closely with the new principal to make sure she supported their efforts. The association also sought support from similar organizations in the area. They spoke with and learned from leaders in other parent associations in Atlanta. The association also got support from families in the area without school-aged children as well as those who were sending their children to private schools. Whether the families were planning on sending children to Avondale Elementary or not, they still supported the idea of a strong neighborhood school.

The AEA has also been successful because they have invested in their own infrastructure. The group has achieved nonprofit status, generally a paperwork nightmare, in order to ensure that they will have greater potential to raise funds. Further, the association is attempting to secure a more flexible structure for how they will work with the school and surrounding community in the future. In addition, they work on the infrastructure of the community by trying to find ways to curb the level of transience among refugees in the area. They believe that the charter school status may help the school get more parents involved and, as a result, encourage them to stay in the area.

The association has also worked diligently on public relations for themselves and for the school. Their Web site (www.aeainfo.org) provides extensive information about the group and about the school. In addition, the association pays for ads in the regular city newsletters and rents a booth at the neighborhood fall art festival to pass out balloons, paint faces, and provide information for current and potential community members. They also host a float in the city's Fourth of July parade so that community members can see them and their work on a regular basis. In addition, they make sure homes that are on the market have brochures available that tell potential homeowners that the local elementary school is a good one and also provides contact information for the association. By sorting out and making public the test scores of the more stable students within the elementary school, parents also provide a better image of the school than parents considering the area would see from the other official reports.

Finally, the AEA has worked diligently to make sure they become and remain a vital element in the operations of the elementary school. We feel this is a critical point in building relationships with schools. The key to the association's viability is to make sure the school and district leaders cannot imagine the school without them. By working to make the school facilities more beautiful, supporting refugee children by providing uniforms, and assisting teachers in writing grants, the association has become a very important part of the school community.

Lessons from the Avondale Education Association

- ✎ Parent associations will not create changes overnight. Meaningful change takes time.

- ✎ Leaders in parent associations need to invest in education and training.

- ✎ Successful parent associations need to invest in their own infrastructure of support.

- ✎ Public relations matter for both the parent association and the school it supports.

- ✎ Parent associations need to become vital factors within the school's operations.

CONCLUSIONS

In this chapter we have attempted to help you imagine what parent involvement might look like in your community. We offered critical information regarding why and how parents get involved, qualities of authentic involvement, and demonstrated ways in which you could use technology to increase the level of involvement of parents. We have also offered some images of parent involvement to help you move beyond the more global or ambiguous charge of getting involved—parent centers, study circles, and local parent associations. To help you visualize your work even more, we provided a detailed account of one parent association in particular—the Avondale Parent Association. We challenge you at this point to envision potential partnerships between parents and community members and your school. What would you hope to achieve based upon that collaboration? Keep these goals in mind as you explore Chapter 8 and work to develop a plan of action where you will be able to achieve your goals.

REFERENCES

Amherst Regional Parent Center, http://www.arhsparentcenter.org/homepage. Retrieved April 15, 2008.

Anderson, G. L. (1998). Toward authentic participation. *American Educational Research Journal*, 35(4), 571–603.

Christie, K. (2005). Changing the nature of parents involvement. *Phi Delta Kappan*, (86)9, 645–646.

Comer, J. (1998). *Waiting for a Miracle: Why Schools Can't Solve Our Problems— and How We Can.* New York: Dutton.

D'Angelo, D. A. and Adler, C. R. (1991). Chapter I: A catalyst for improving parent involvement. *Phi Delta Kappan*, 75(5), 350–354.

Davies, D. (1991). Schools reaching out: Families, school and community. *Phi Delta Kappan*, 75(5), 376–382.

Deslangdes, Rollande and Bertrand, Richard. (2005). Motivation of Parent Involvement in Secondary-Level Schooling. *The Journal of Educational Research*, 98(3), 164–176.

Giles, H. C. (1998). Parent engagement as a school reform strategy. *ERIC Digest*, No. 135.

Halsey, P. A. (2005). Parent involvement in junior high schools: A failure to communicate. *American Secondary Education*, 34(1), 57–69.

Hoover-Dempsey, K. V., Bassler, O. C., and Brissie, J. S. (1992). Explorations in parent-school relations. *The Journal of Educational Research*, 85, 287–294.

Hoover-Dempsey, K. V. and Sandler, H. M. (1997). Why to parents become involved in their children's education? *Review of Educational Research*, 67, 3–42.

Montgomery County Study Circles Program, http://www.montgomeryschoolsmd.org/departments/studycircles/. Retrieved April 15, 2008.

Sohn, Soomin and Wang, X. C. (2006). Immigrant parents' involvement in American schools: Perspectives from Korean mothers. *Early Childhood Education Journal,* 34(2), 125–132.

Swap, S. M. (1990). Comparing three philosophies of home-school collaboration. *Equity and Choice,* 5(3), 9–19.

CHAPTER 8

Agents of Change: Enacting the Conversation

WHY GET INVOLVED?

It may be safe to assume that you are interested in making a difference in your school and community by virtue of the fact that you chose this book to read and that you are still reading it through to the last chapter. You may have been concerned about an issue or the general state of well-being of your local school and/or community for some time and have decided to do something about it. You may have moved to an area and know that the school and community could be better based on your experiences elsewhere. Maybe you are a parent whose child has recently entered the school system, and now that you are part of the system, you see concerns and want to get involved. Whatever is your motivation, we believe your choice to get involved is a critical one.

If at this point you are still experiencing doubts, we want to provide additional information that may provide even more incentive for you to get involved in your community. There are a number of reasons why your involvement could make a difference for your community and its schools. First, your involvement could result in more resources for your community and its schools. School districts as well as state and city governmental agencies operate under limited budgets. They typically have to set priorities for how they will allocate resources. If a community does not make a concerted effort to request funds for specific needs, then it is highly unlikely that they will get the resources. In other words, it does not hurt to ask, but if you do not ask, you will not receive. Second, when you get involved in your community and when you help to get others involved, you are more likely to be the ones who make or at least help make decisions in your community. When talking about curriculum decisions with Wells Foshay, a late curriculum scholar, he commented with the following simple but appropriate assessment, "The higher up the decision is made, the dumber the decision." When a community gets involved in its own well-being, it is far more likely that the decisions about the community's future will be better than if they are made by others.

Third, and we believe even more importantly, your involvement will help build a sense of community. A number of researchers have noted how the general population today has become more and more private. We do not engage with others in public. When we do go out and associate with others, it is often with a small group of individuals much like us. Think about your experiences at the grocery store, when you go to vote, or at any other public area. To what degree do you feel connected to those around you? Do you find yourself avoiding eye contact with people you do not know? You may even experience this sense in your own neighborhood, apartment or condominium complex, or in local parks and other public spaces. It is often difficult for individuals to take the initiative to connect with those around them in public spaces, but if you embark on a community project of planning and change, you create a space where members of your community can come together and feel connected. They will have a reason to make eye contact, to talk with one another, and to get to know one another.

Fourth, if you create this space for planning and change, then you will see a change in people themselves. Individuals who otherwise may have felt they had nothing to offer others may see that they are valuable members of the community. You may find that individuals who felt defeated and marginalized may begin to realize change is possible and that they can be part of bringing about that change. When people feel they can make a difference in their communities, it may affect how they maintain their own homes and relationships. This is why you will often see a decline in vandalism and crime in communities that become more active.

Fifth, your involvement will bring about positive changes that you did not anticipate or include in the goals for your actual change process. As the community gets more involved, individuals within the community may see additional ways they can support the community and schools. For example, a business owner may realize he or she could change some practice or expand some service based upon what he or she has learned through the community planning process. While these changes were not part of the community planning steering committee's plans, they may be consistent with and supportive of those plans and thus add value to the process itself.

Finally, your efforts may create a process that will continue in the future— whether you have an active role in future efforts or not. Establishing and supporting a meaningful process for change will hopefully create a sustaining culture of change within the community. If enough people have been involved in the process and if their capacity for leadership is nurtured within the process, then these others may step up in the future to carry on the work you began.

Why Get Involved?

🖎 More resources for your school and community

🖎 Localize decision making

🖎 Stronger sense of community

🖎 Increased esteem of community members

🖎 Value-added improvements

🖎 Greater potential for a culture of change

THE PLANNING PROCESS: COMMUNITY AUDIT FOR CHANGE

So, we have convinced you that you need to get involved. You are ready to jump in and create a process for your community to try to bring about change within the schools. We want to share a process for promoting community change because schools cannot be seen in a vacuum. If you only seek to bring about change in the school and ignore the needs, opportunities, and resources within your community, you will compromise the potential good you can do. Making your school concerns actually community concerns also offers a powerful counter-discourse in the midst of the No Child Left Behind (NCLB) rhetoric blaming schools for all social ills. With this in mind, what do you do next? Keep in mind that what we suggest is not a prescriptive process. We offer possible steps for the strategic planning and change process. Based on your community and the examples you have explored in other communities, you may find alternative processes that are more appropriate for your efforts.

Step One: Identify Participants

First, you will want to get others involved. Often, as was the case in the Avondale Education Association, initial involvement comes through word of mouth. However, we caution you to make sure whatever means you use to get people involved do not exclude critical stakeholders in the community. If you rely on word of mouth and that word of mouth happens in exclusive places alone (i.e., at pools with expensive membership fees, etc.) then critical stakeholders will be excluded. Find multiple ways to let community members know about the planning and change project. Meet with key community members who may help get the word out—business owners, local politicians, church leaders, community activists, social support networks, other organizations, etc. In addition to providing the initial information about a chance for individuals to get involved, we strongly encourage you to have some way to communicate the variety of ways individuals will be able to get involved and what you generally hope to accomplish (i.e., to improve schools and community, etc.). You want to be specific enough for individuals to imagine themselves helping, but you do not want to get too specific, or individuals will feel as if they are just joining in to support someone else's vision of the school and community.

Be careful to include multiple ways for people to express an interest in getting involved. If you have a housing project in your community, designate a contact person or provide a sign-up sheet for individuals to express their interest. Also, provide a phone number and an e-mail address to allow individuals to express an interest in a way that is most convenient. Once you get a list of individuals who are interested, you should follow up with each of them to discern their level of interest. It may be worthwhile for you to develop an interest inventory form that you can fill out for each potential participant to determine their level of interest, their availability, and any skills and knowledge they may have that would contribute to the process. Based upon the interest expressed, you may need to seek out additional support. Some individuals may not express an interest because they feel that it will be taken care of by others. As we mentioned elsewhere, some individuals may not contact you because they feel they have nothing to contribute. Others may not volunteer because of their schedules or other conflicts—without realizing they would have opportunities to participate without having to commit to regular meetings. All in all, the more effort you put into getting people involved, the more diverse and dynamic your participants will be. Ultimately, you will want to not only have a list of willing participants, but you will also want to determine who among them can and are willing to serve in a steering committee function and who may choose to spearhead or chair potential subcommittees. Much of the substructure of the group will not be determined until priorities are set, but to the greater the degree you can get an early commitment, the more likely you will have people willing to get involved from the beginning.

Step Two: Define Goals

Second, once you identify those who wish to be involved, you need to define goals for the group. This may be tricky if you have a large number of potential participants. We would suggest that you begin with some sort of community planning forum. This meeting would be open to the public and would probably last two to three hours. Provide some time at the beginning for people to get to know one another and to get comfortable with the space. Then open the forum with open-ended questions that let individuals to share what they feel matters most in their community and school and what they would like to see as priorities for the planning and change initiative. It is critical that the facilitator(s) of this meeting listen to the participants. From the initial sharing and brainstorming, identify important themes and use next part of the meeting to break into small groups to discuss the themes. While the logistics may be a challenge, we would encourage you to let the participants self-select the small groups they want to join so they can spend their time discussing the issues of greatest importance to them. Ultimately, if you have a theme where no one expresses an interest, then it is probably not a high priority any way. Try to have general guidelines available (in print) so that the small groups have some guidance. Ideally, if you have enough individuals involved in planning the community forum, you could have someone designated for each small group to help facilitate the conversations. After giving the group enough time to discuss the issues in small groups, then reconvene and have the facilitator or a volunteer from each group to share what their small group discussed. As small groups share, take notes and try to identify themes and connections between groups. Also allow others in the forum to share the themes, ideas, connections, and additional questions they may note during the discussion. Creating an open forum like this provides a good starting point for defining purposes for your group. Yet, it is just the first step. Other measures will be important—particularly to involve those who may not have been able to attend the forum.

What ways could you share the outcomes of the open forum with your community? One way would be to post the notes online. This would provide a record of your work, and it would be useful particularly if it could be linked to a community Web site. Again, as we cautioned before, this may exclude individuals who do not have access to the Internet. Another possibility would be to also post the information in a public place. Does the community have a center where people gather? Does the local housing project have a common area where people come together? Perhaps your community's primary shared space is a local grocery store. Whatever those spaces are, you may be able to post the issues and priorities that came out of the initial meeting. In addition to sharing information, you could also use the postings to gather additional information and priorities from community members. What if you were to list the goals of the group with a space where individuals could indicate their preferences? In many strategic planning meetings, groups will post goals on large pieces of paper and then give individuals a certain number of stickers to paste on those goals that mean the most to them. Those goals with the most stickers become the biggest priorities. With a little creative thinking, you may be able to replicate this in community centers, public libraries, churches, and other important centers of your community. This will let community members know that even though they cannot or choose not to get involved in the planning process, their opinions still matter.

Step Three: Determining Priorities and Boundaries

By this time you have hopefully determined a steering committee or some core groups from your list of volunteers who will then interpret the findings from the brainstorming and priority setting processes. You will want to keep in mind the scope of your efforts when determining priorities. All of the ideas presented in the open forum may be worthy, but you will not be able to address them all. More than just picking the items that had the most "stickers" or other signs of priority, you will also want to make sure the initiatives you choose fit together and support one another. Particularly since your primary focus is the school, you will want to make sure the social issues that you select have some direct relationship with the schools and the issues within the school that you are addressing. You may find other critical issues within the community that may or may not have as much of an effect on the school. While these are also important, you will want to table them or suggest that some other group deal with those issues while you focus on school-related concerns. At any rate, once you recognize priorities for the group, you will need to set boundaries for the group. What are you realistically able to accomplish within a year or two? If there are concerns that will take several years to address, how can you respond to elements of the issue without focusing solely on such a long-range project that you may lose interest and momentum from those interested in working toward change?

Step Four: Gather Data

Once you have identified participants, prioritized purposes, and defined your boundaries or the scope of your efforts, you then need to determine what information you need in order to make recommendations for change. As we mentioned in Chapter 5, the only way to achieve meaningful change in your schools and community is to respond to authentic data. To begin, you need to identify what you already know about your schools and community. While this seems obvious, often data about a community is scattered according to whatever agency or party collected it. As much as possible, find out as much as you can about your community and school. Take advantage of school district data, census data, city statistics, etc. One challenge you may find is that the data you find may cover more or less ground than your specific community. For example, you may find crime rates for the entire city of Indianapolis when you want to find them specifically for the area known as Broad Ripple. When this happens, you have to be cautious to not generalize from the larger body of data. Realize that in some instances you may not be able to get the information you need. Do not hesitate to ask local officials for help when collecting data. They may have information at their disposal that they are willing to share that otherwise might take you countless hours to find. Other local resources for community data would include real estate agents, visitor and convention bureaus, and chambers of commerce. Your local library may have reports or data about the area available as well.

From this initial level of awareness, you will be able to generate meaningful questions or areas for inquiry that will guide the next steps. Your steering committee should determine whether the areas for potential inquiry match with your stated priorities—to ensure that you are not just pursuing the data that is easiest or most interesting to gather. Once you have determined the critical areas to study, you then need to also make sure the scope of the collective inquiry is reasonable for your timeline. You then need to determine the best means through which you can gather the necessary information. In Chapter 5 we outlined five ways to collect data about your school and community: artifacts, systematic observations, focus groups, interviews, and surveys. While we will not repeat what we described in that chapter, we offer images of what these varied forms of inquiry might provide for research when the focus in on the school within the context of its community.

What artifacts might you find within your community? Consider this, what if your whole community froze in time as if it were some sort of science fiction scene? What if individuals from another planet or from another time in history descended upon this frozen community? What would they assume about you? What would they identify as the priorities and values of your community? Whatever trail we leave—whether over time or if frozen in time—provides evidence of what matters to us. Minutes from city council or city commissioner meetings reveal a great deal about a community and its values. The pattern of businesses that have started, failed, remained, and relocated also say something about a community. What can you find in local newspapers that may provide insights into the community and its relationship with its schools? What local events—fairs, festivals, etc.—indicate something about the community? To what degree, if any, were schools involved in these events? Where will individuals find critical information about a community? For example, in one of the author's urban communities, the city manager sends out regular e-mails about missing pets, break-ins, and other helpful information. While this information is very valuable to a number of the members of the community, only those who have Internet access have access to the information that may keep them safe and help them find their lost pets. Not only does the e-mail communication conveys something about the community—that it is a fairly close-knit and small community within an urban area that can stay connected about local things—it also points to a problematic system that provides information to more of its middle- and upper-middle-class residents than to those who live in the low-rent apartments and housing projects.

Second, how can a community group use systematic observations to learn something about the schools and the community? Systematic observations seem obvious in schools, but they can also provide valuable information in the community about the community and its relationship with the schools. For example, in visiting a small elementary school in an urban area, one of the authors was surprised to find the number of parents waiting to walk their children home at the end of the day. In particular, there were a large number of fathers standing on the front lawn of the school waiting for their children. Based on this author's observation, that urban school had a wonderful opportunity to get parents involved who were coming to the school twice a day and who seemed to have some degree of flexibility in their work schedules to be able to do so. In addition, by virtue of the fact that so many of the students in the school walked to and from school there would appear to be greater potential to build a sense of community than if they were picked up in cars and drove to their homes. Walking to and from school provides more opportunities for conversations with others, and increased conversations and increased connections with each other can lead to a greater sense of community. Another example of using observations includes when a community "sees" the students from the school. In a number of urban areas, the schools are located in and around areas with parks, museums, courthouses, etc. How often do the students visit these resources around their schools? Do you ever see lines of children walking with their teachers and parent volunteers to hear an outdoor concert? To what degree do stores, libraries, and other businesses in the area display artwork from the schools or otherwise acknowledge that the school is part of the community? These examples are just a few of the ways observations can provide valuable information about the school in relation to its community.

Focus groups are a third source of valuable information in your community. As we mentioned before, some individuals may feel that they cannot commit to a long-term commitment for parent group. Yet, they may be willing to sit down and talk about concerns that interest them. Using focus groups can help your organization gather a variety of information from community members. While we will not repeat the steps in planning and implementing focus groups that are outlined in Chapter 5, we will suggest that you take advantage of community gathering places for form and conduct focus groups in your area. While these gathering places may not have the diversity that we suggested in Chapter 5, they will be convenient groups where you can gather valuable information. For example, you could speak to a group at a senior citizen's center or at a homeless shelter. These specific groups may not feel comfortable going into a school or other public spaces and speaking with a variety of individuals from the community. You could also speak to church groups or civic organizations or hold sessions in coffee shops or other locations where community members tend to gather. Focus groups are a great way to collect opinions, ideas, and feelings of a number of community members. It is also a way to demonstrate to the community that their views matter.

A fourth way to gather information about the school and community is interviews. Because interviews are very time intensive, we would encourage you to identify key individuals who may have a wide range of insights from which you could learn. For example, a city planner, manager of a social services office, minister, or political official may offer insights that he or she has gained by virtue of his or her position. When you combine focus group meetings with interviews with key individuals, you may be able to get a better picture of an issue. For example, a focus group may express frustrations over a particular policy in the community. While they may give their opinions on the policy and its effects, they may not know the context in which the policy was made or the rationale for why the policy was implemented. By interviewing a city manager or city council member, you may be able to learn that the policy was put into place because of other concerns within the community. By using both focus groups and interviews, you are then able to learn more about the policy and its effects.

A final source of data collection we will suggest is surveys. As we mentioned in Chapter 5, surveys can be helpful if you want to get views from your entire community. One challenge you will have when you are planning a survey with the whole community instead of just the school is that you will need to determine an appropriate sample. Depending upon the size of your community, you will not be able to survey everyone, so how do you choose an appropriate sample population? As we have mentioned in other contexts, you will also want to make sure the survey is accessible to as many individuals as possible. You may find that some individuals in your community may be reluctant to complete the survey—particularly some immigrant populations who may fear harassment from officials if they provide contact information. In order to encourage wide participation in the survey, you will need to find ways where people can answer the questions in a safe environment. You will also want to make sure those who are asked to answer the survey can understand it. If individuals struggle with reading or with English, they may feel intimidated and not complete the survey. We mentioned in Chapter 5 that schools have opportunities where parents come to the school (i.e., parent conferences) and as are more likely to complete the survey. Can you think of times when members of the community are together and perhaps waiting for something, so they may be willing to complete the survey to pass the time?

We encourage you to keep your scope in mind when developing surveys. While it may seem like a good idea to develop a number of surveys to gather a variety of information, keep in mind that you will need to do something with all of the data you collect, so too many surveys can ultimately become a problem. Also, we encourage you to publish the results of the surveys—whether on a Web site or in a local paper—to show community members that you followed through with the survey and that you will use the information you gathered. This may provide the incentive they will need if you send out a different survey for them to complete.

Collecting data is a comprehensive and time consuming process that takes substantial resources. As we mentioned in Chapter 5, you will want to seek resources to support your efforts. Community members, businesses, and civic associations may be willing to support this work because it will ultimately benefit them as well. In addition, grants and other state and local initiatives may provide necessary support. We encourage you to seek out resources in your community and in the city at large to provide the training you will need in order for community members to be involved in the inquiry process. Local universities and businesses may be willing to support the training of individuals in order to help. Keep in mind that the training and planning are critical before you actually begin to design your research and gather data. It is also important to review the research that has been done elsewhere and involves similar issues in order to learn from the larger body of research out there. You may find that researchers or other community organizations in other regions may have engaged in some of the same kind of research you are considering, and you may be able to use instruments they developed or develop your studies with their work in mind.

Step Five: Analyze Data

Once you have collected the data, you need to determine what it means and how it is significant based upon your goals. In many cases, researchers gather a great deal of data and then merely organize it rather than analyze it. Organizing data merely requires you to put it in a usable form. While this is somewhat worthwhile, it does not maximize the potential of your efforts. After organizing the data, you need to seek themes, connections, contradictions, and concerns. Foremost in your thinking should be "so what?" What is the significance of the information you have collected? What do you learn when you consider one set of information with another? We suggest that you form teams of individuals who can look at the data with critical eyes, have them explore the "so what" of the information, and then discuss their findings with others to see if others identify different issues and implications. We also encourage you to use whatever system you have developed to communicate progress of the group to the public and publish your results and conclusions at this site. Give the community the opportunity to challenge your conclusions or ask questions that may enrich your exploration. Include within your conclusions whatever questions remain after you have completed your current line of inquiry—either questions you were not able to address in your research or questions that emerged because of your research.

Step Six: Generate Conclusions and Recommendations

Ultimately your steering committee will need to generate conclusions and recommendations based upon the results of your research and the responses from the community about those results. When you generate recommendations, you will want to make sure they are aligned with your original aims and goals for the project. Glaring issues may have emerged from the research that are not part of what you determined to be the original scope of your work. If that happens, you want to acknowledge the concerns and propose that the current group or another group address them in the future rather than compromising your original goals and addressing the issue in a superficial manner. While the actual recommendations should be generated from those most involved in the overall process, namely, the steering committee, the recommendations should be informed by group and community feedback, and they should be made public with clear rationales. Once the recommendations are made, we encourage you to hold another open forum and allow community members and those who have been involved in the parent group to respond.

Step Seven: Act

The inquiry process may have taken you months to complete, and at this point we imagine that you are feeling fatigued. Nevertheless, you need to remember that you were gathering information for a reason—to make changes in your school. Based upon the priorities you set in the beginning, the data you have generated, and the potential resources you may have, you need to develop plans of action for change. Identify key players for the initiatives and timelines for achieving certain goals. You will have to make sure the initiatives you plan are consistent with the district, state, and federal guidelines. If you feel that pressures applied through the high-stakes assessment culture will undermine critical initiatives, then you need to develop ways to fight the current restrictions in order to accomplish your goals. We anticipate that you will struggle with doing what you know is right and what you see is possible in the current climate. Do not give up hope. Apply pressure where necessary, and be diligent in your efforts. Further, as you approach key points in your timeline for change, make sure you assess your own progress. If you have not made the kind of progress you had hoped, then try to determine what factors may be hindering your efforts. Further, we encourage you to make your achievements public. Keep updates posted online and in other accessible areas so that community members do not forget what you are doing and see that their efforts in the process have helped bring about desired results. Finally, take time out to celebrate your achievements—do not wait until the change or reform is "done." Realize that change is a slow process and every level of progress is worthy of celebration. This will help you maintain your momentum and commitment for the long haul ahead.

Community Planning for Change

✎ Identify participants

✎ Define goals

✎ Determine priorities and boundaries

✎ Gather Data

✎ Analyze Data

✎ Generate conclusions and recommendations

✎ Act

DYNAMICS OF COMMUNITY PLANNING

The Academy for Sustainable Communities in conjunction with the Royal Town Planning Institute Community Planning Project and the Department for Communities and Local Government in England have developed an extensive Web site for community planning (www.communityplanning.net). They provide valuable information for parents who are hoping to organize for change in schools and communities. This site provides many factors to consider when organizing to bring about change in your community and school. We will try to outline a number of them here and explore how they relate to a strategic planning committee for school change.

First, when you establish a steering committee of core group of stakeholders that will be responsible for your community audit and action plan, you will need to establish rules and boundaries. In all likelihood, you will experience conflict throughout the process. It is critical that all stakeholders play a part in setting up the rules and processes for conflict resolution as well as what the group will do when a conflict cannot be resolved. Will the group determine that there may be times when individuals will be asked to leave the group? It is also important to recognize and talk about issues of power within the group. Is there a hierarchy within the group? If so, why? Does the steering committee have any level of decision-making power that others do not? How do you make sure diverse ideas are heard and considered? While there may be a primary facilitator who gets everyone involved, it is critical that these issues be resolved and processes put in place by as many of the stakeholders as possible to ensure that they will support the processes when issues arise. It may also serve your group well to identify an outsider who can step in if needed. This person should have experience in conflict resolution, and it should be someone who can step in and objectively help the group out. In other words, it should be an outside consultant you would pay or otherwise compensate versus someone's cousin who will step in and help out if needed.

Second, realize that people who get involved will have different agendas. Some business leaders may hope that by getting involved they will get more business. Any local politicians may get involved in hopes of gaining more support in the next election. Some family members may get involved in order to feel important or gain some level of social power or control. Trying to force participants to come to the table with the same agenda will be futile. What is critical, however, is to be mindful of any agendas that serve as a destructive force in the process. Be prepared to handle problems that may emerge as you begin in the process. Have some sort of plan for anyone who is preventing the group from moving forward. You want to make sure the manner in which you identify problems does not rest solely in one person. It helps to have clear guidelines created by the stakeholders that address what happens when conflict emerges—how to try to resolve it and what to do when it cannot be resolved.

Third, recognize that your project will have limitations. You will not be able to address every concern within your school and your community. You will need to set realistic boundaries when you plan to make sure you move toward meaningful change. This is why it is critical in the planning stage to set priorities and stick to what you identify as your primary purposes. Anticipate that you will discover additional and perhaps larger concerns, but keep in mind that getting sidetracked will, in all likelihood, prevent you from achieving your original goals. Also keep in mind that this process can be continually renewing. If additional concerns bubble up in the research process, then you can address those concerns in the next cycle of strategic planning.

Fourth, accept the fact that different people involved in the process will have different levels of commitment. Not everyone who may sign up for work in the process will be as excited about the process or as willing to give up time to participate. In addition, some individuals may be highly committed and excited about the project, but they may have such busy schedules that they cannot give as much time as you would like. Avoid judging individuals for the varied commitments unless their level of commitment becomes an obstacle in the process. If that happens, use the processes you have developed for conflict resolution. In addition, we strongly recommend that you create opportunities for involvement at varied levels. Some individuals may prefer to serve on a specific ad hoc committee that is very busy for a short period of time and then done. Others may prefer to jump in and help at one point or another without being part of the larger steering committee. As we mentioned with involvement in schools, some may be able to help online but because of work schedules or childcare issues may not be able to meet regularly. The more you can create varied opportunities for involvement, the more individuals you are likely to get involved and the more support you will likely get in the end when making recommendations.

Fifth, it is important that the members of the group are honest with each other about motivations, opinions, and community connections, and that the group itself functions transparently. Hidden agendas can destroy a group's efforts by destroying the trust. If members of a steering committee are constantly questioning the motives of other members, then they will not be addressing the actual concerns in an authentic manner. Similarly, if others involved in the process question the motives of the steering committee, then they will be less likely to get involved and provide help where they are needed. Even if they do help, they may very well question and challenge the recommendations that come from the steering committee and then all the efforts of the process have been in vain. We mentioned Wikispaces in Chapter 7 where the entire community could view the planning process as well as the information the group gathers. We would strongly encourage you to not only post schedules and updates regarding the planning and change process, but you should also maintain open invitations to meetings as much as possible. If you post the meetings for steering committees and subgroups and indicate that all community members are invited to attend, you send a powerful message that you have nothing to hide. We do not think you will have to worry about crowd control. Most people will, in all likelihood, be too busy to attend many of the meetings. However, if you have establish rules for the meeting—much like schools boards do for their meetings allowing visitors a limited time to express their opinions—then you show you are responsive to community concerns while maintaining the integrity of the planning process. If the steering group uses something like this, it would help support the transparency of the process because others could see the decision-making process.

Sixth, it is important that the group be visionary but realistic when setting boundaries. Change happens when you try to achieve an image of how things can be different or better. Yet, setting goals too high will lead to frustration and ultimately to failure. Keeping in mind that the group will have different motivations and levels of commitment, setting appropriate yet visionary goals may be more of a challenge than you first think. As you proceed, you may realize the goals you set were too lofty and determine that you need to scale back. You may also determine that your goals were too modest and that you need to challenge yourselves further.

Seventh, when planning extensive efforts to bring about change, you need to be mindful of and find ways to build local capacity. How can you develop both the human and social capital of your community? What local skills are needed in order to proceed with improving your community and school? Let members of the community help identify these needs and make suggestions on how to provide this sort of support. Otherwise those in "power" in the steering committee take on a paternal image—knowing best what community members need and providing it for them. Community members should not only be involved in identifying needs, they should also be involved in providing solutions—organizing community training, literacy programs, etc. It is also important to make sure capacity building does not become a series of discrete and disjointed projects. How can your community create coherence in its renewal and development? How does the investment in capacity help support your aims for the community and school? To the degree that you can show what you are doing to build capacity and how it relates to your aims, you will communicate to the community and school that your efforts are deliberate, meaningful, and critical for community development.

Eighth, communication is critical in any change process. If you do not develop and support effective means of communication, your entire strategic planning process will be compromised. As you can imagine at this point, your efforts—particularly if they are as comprehensive as we describe here—will involve a large number of people doing a large number of different things—some of which will overlap and influence one another. In the end, you hope to have a coherent and cohesive plan for improving your school and community. How do you achieve coherence in the midst of all the different things going on? Even if the primary facilitator has a handle on all the different pieces, you could still end up with what appears to be a disjointed mess unless communication is clear throughout the process. Keep human nature in mind. On the whole, people do not always listen well, and at times, people have "selective hearing." Even when people do listen, they often forget those things that do not necessarily apply to them at that point and time. When issues or plans do concern them, they may ignore them because of pressing concerns and intend to go back to them once some other immediate concern in their lives is over. Again, we encourage using Wikispaces or some online equivalent to a Web site to keep issues current. We encourage you to post meeting days, times, and locations on the site because people will forget to write them down. Otherwise, the key facilitator and steering committee members will be constantly bombarded with phone calls and e-mails asking about the details of meetings and when things are due. In addition, if you post this information and keep it updated, it lets other community members know what you are doing and will provide them with valuable information if they choose to attend the meetings.

Ninth, it is critical that you pace yourselves in the planning and change process. While you may be anxious to see change quickly, rushing can create problems and undermine your efforts. However, if you do not set deadlines for yourself then the process can drag on without anything being accomplished. Balance is important. While there is no particular set pace, you may want to review how other communities brought about change and pay close attention to the pace at which they accomplished the change. Once you have reviewed various scenarios, you then consider your community dynamics as well as the urgency of some of the changes. Of course, the scale of your aims will also influence this significantly. If you have set broad and lofty goals, then keep in mind it will take longer to achieve them. Also keep in mind that you may have to table some concerns until a later date if they are preventing you from moving forward with other concerns and/or your overall aims. Much like those who use the Stephen Covey planning process shift things from one "to do" list to another with arrows, you may have to shift some of your concerns to a future cycle of the planning and change process.

Tenth, make sure your planning and decision making fit with the larger governmental structures, policies, and procedures. It will do no good to develop change initiatives for your community if they are in conflict with state, city, or school district policies. This may be a bigger challenge than you imagine, and it may force you to approximate an ideal you have if the current political structure prevents you from making the changes the way you want to. Do your research to see if there are any mechanisms within the level of governance causing the conflict or a higher level of governance that may provide alternatives for you. For example, as we mentioned in the example of the Avondale Education Association, Georgia has passed legislation allowing districts to apply for charter status. This status would free districts from some of the state-level constraints. If your state has a similar provision, it may be worthwhile to pressure your school district to explore this option or to identify ways in which your needs can be met within the current structure. While many districts may not want to take advantage of new provisions such as the charter status, knowing that those options exist may put them in a position where they have to be more willing to respond to needs of parents and community members.

Eleventh, involve as many people as possible in the planning process. It is very tempting to start work once you have a core body of volunteers. Even if you begin the process at that point, you need to ask yourselves, "Who is not at the table? Whose voice is not being heard?" You may discover that a group that feels marginalized in your community did not get involved because they felt their contributions would not be valued or they may not have had access to the information about the process when you were seeking participants. You may also have others in the community who may not want to be involved but who will have definite opinions about the work once all is said and done. As frustrating as that scenario is, you can realistically anticipate some degree of resistance from individuals who chose to stay out of the process. If you send out updates (preferably in the language of the community member) and ask community members for feedback throughout the process, you will be able to address multiple needs. First, you will be able to keep those who are uncomfortable with participating involved. In addition, you will be able respond to those end-of-process critics by saying they had an opportunity throughout the process to voice their concerns and offer alternatives.

Twelfth, we strongly encourage you to network with other community associations and learn from their efforts. We mentioned previously that you should look at the work of other groups to determine the pace of your change. We also encourage you to maintain a network with other parent and community groups and share your processes with one another. Not only will you learn from these other groups, you will also be able to support their work by sharing what you have learned from your own efforts. Seek out community groups in other urban areas to share ideas. Many of these groups will have information available through Web sites. This would be an example of how someone in the community who is too busy to attend meetings may be able to search for these other groups online and provide contact information for the steering committee or for some subcommittee designated to network with other associations.

Thirteenth, plan for ways to maintain momentum with your efforts. In long planning and changing processes, people can experience organizational fatigue. How do you maintain the necessary level of energy and commitment over the weeks and months of work? We would encourage you to plan times where you pause in the process, celebrate your accomplishments, and otherwise just take a breath. If every meeting together involves rushing about and trying to get X, Y, and Z accomplished, then your relationships with one another will break down. Every once in a while hold a social function where you take time out to get to know one another better. You may also want to have social time every once in a while at a local eatery or coffee shop with the expectation that you are not getting together with an agenda and the only outcome is to have fun together. These events will help build relationships and provide fun memories to help you get through the more difficult times. They may also help in terms of minimizing conflict in the future because people may begin to trust each other more when they get to know one another.

Fourteenth, it is critical that you respect diversity within your process. Your community, in all likelihood, represents very diverse cultures and a wealth of local knowledge. You need to be responsive to your community's diversity, and you need to determine an effective way to keep your responsiveness in check throughout the process. You may feel that by simply including diverse individuals on the planning committees that you automatically guarantee that you are sensitive to diversity. Simply having your community's diverse population represented on the committees is not enough. Groups can fall into groupthink where ideas take on lives of their own. When you develop your inquiry methods through which you will gather information, you need to make sure you are representing the whole community and respecting the local knowledge of the community. For example, if you design a survey, how will you ensure that those who cannot read will also be able to respond? If your community has a significant population of illiterate adults, you will want to make sure their interests and needs are met as well. Throughout the process you need to stop at times and think, "Whose values are and are not represented in our work up to this point?" Further, whenever you get to a point of pause—whether it is when you are analyzing a particular set of information or generating formative conclusions based on information collected at a point and time, you need to assess the degree to which your work represents the whole community. Including diverse views and local knowledge will make your process messier and more time consuming, but we believe it absolutely critical that you honor and respect all who make up your community.

Finally, we believe you should invest resources in this process. Unless you have someone who is able to treat this process much like a full-time job and truly capable of facilitating the complex process, then you may need to hire a key facilitator to monitor and maintain the process. If you do hire a key facilitator, then it will be critical to make sure he or she does not take over the project and undermine the communal nature of the work. Otherwise, honestly assess what your community members are able to do well and efficiently and then identify areas where you may need to hire outside consultants. We realize it may be difficult to justify outside consultants to members of your community, but keep in mind that lack of expertise will slow down or derail your efforts.

If you have ever watched the television programs where individuals "flip" homes for profit, you will see a clear example of this. Time and time again in these shows individuals choose to do something themselves rather than hiring an expert—whether it is painting cabinets rather than having them refinished professionally or putting in their own plumbing or electrical systems. If you have seen these shows then you have seen how in many of these instances the individuals end up losing money because of the amount of time it took them to do it themselves or because they did it poorly and the house did not pass inspection. The same concerns apply for community planning. Choosing to do something yourself could cost you time or success in the process.

In order to secure resources for hiring outside consultants we encourage you to first see if individuals or businesses in the community are willing to invest in the process themselves. You may find that individuals or businesses would prefer to donate money to the process rather than get involved in the meetings. Further, businesses are more used to engaging in strategic planning, so they may be more willing to invest in a planning process for the city. They may also have "human resources" there in the community or in the larger business that you can use in the process. In addition, we encourage you to see grant support to help pay for the consultants. First look at the city and the state to see if they have initiatives that would help you. You may also want to ask them and the school district if they could provide financial support since this process will benefit them greatly. In each of these cases, you will need to provide a clear description of the process and what you hope to accomplish. Taking time to develop a presentation will increase the likelihood that you will get support. Fundraisers are also an option, although we discourage you from relying on them. Parents and community members may be willing to buy some brownies or wrapping paper if they can "see" where the money is going (i.e., a new playground, books for a library, etc.). They may be more reluctant to support fundraising from something as ambiguous as a planning and change process. Further, fundraising takes time and energy—often with a very small return. Be particularly wary of the fundraising companies that promise large returns. There is a reason why they are in the "business" of fundraising. You are far more likely to make a large profit for them rather than raising a great deal of money for yourself.

What Should You Consider When Planning for Change?

- Establish rules and boundaries for the process.

- Recognize and accept different agendas for participation.

- Recognize and maintain limitations for your current planning and change process.

- Create opportunities for individuals with different levels of commitment to participate.

- Be honest with each other and transparent with your process.

- Be visionary but realistic when setting boundaries.

- Build local capacity for your planning and change process.

- Develop and support effective communication.

- Pace yourself throughout the process.

- Make sure your work fits with the larger governmental structures, policies, and procedures.

- Involve as many people as possible in the planning process.

- Network with other community associations and learn from their efforts.

- Plan for ways to maintain momentum with your efforts.

- Respect diversity with your process.

- Invest resources in your process.

CONCLUSIONS

The purpose of this book has been to help you bring about meaningful and sustainable change in your local school. We have attempted to introduce you to the history of school reform as well as current policies and legislation and how it plays out in urban schools. We have also introduced you to basic concepts in leadership and organizational theory as well as basic principles of data collection and analysis. To try to make the ideas more concrete, we have also offered you images of success—both Mission Hill School in Boston and the Avondale Education Association in Atlanta. You may feel that we have armed you with just enough to make you dangerous. We hope we have helped you to envision possibilities for your school and community and have provided some of the basic knowledge and skills that you will need to act upon your vision.

We organized this book into three sections—an introduction, a section for educators, and a section for parents, guardians, and community members. By doing this we in no way imply that stakeholders should not work together. Ideally, efforts to bring about change in your school will involve all stakeholders and they will be supported by those in leadership positions in the district, city, and state. However, if one group seems unresponsive, we urge you to proceed anyway. Always try to build support from all stakeholders, but do not let a school leader, a community leader, or any state official prevent you from your aims. Any work toward building community and improving schools can make a difference for urban children, their families, and the community.

REFERENCES

Center for Governmental Studies. (2004). *Northwest Illinois Workforce Investment Board Community Audit*. DeKalb, IL: Northern Illinois University.

Hawtin, M., Hughes, G., Percy-Smith, J. (1994). *Community Profiling: Auditing Social Needs*. London: Open University Press.

Wates, N. (2000). *The Community Planning Handbook*. London: Earthscan Publications, Ltd.

Workforce Learning Strategies. (2000). *Conducting a Community Audit: Assessing the Workforce Development Needs and Resources of Your Community*. Washington, DC: U.S. Department of Labor.

Glossary

Aggregation. An organizational element where the work of individuals within an organization can emerge into singular but collective acts.

Artifacts. Data that include valuable evidence found within the context in which one is researching. In schools, artifacts include meeting notes, parent sign-in sheets, bulletin board displays, etc.

Bureaucratic accountability. A form of accountability that rests on procedural, top-down directives.

Butterfly effect. An idea in organizational theory that points to how small changes within an organization can have very significant and unintended outcomes.

Civic capacity. A condition that requires accepting one's role within a community and seeing what needs to be done as a civic obligation. It represents the ability, knowledge, and skills by which urban stakeholders can accept their civic responsibility in participating in the reform of the community—and this includes education.

Community Audit. A process in which individuals systematically examine their community to identify needs and issues as well as resources.

Complex adaptive systems (CAS). A view of organizations that considers the complex and unpredictable nature of how people and institutions interact.

Curriculum wars. Debates and conflicts primarily fond in states with large immigrant populations. The 1990s curriculum wars were waged over what it means to be "American," as well as how the history of America should be taught.

Educational Management Organizations. Also known as EMOs, these forms of school management are being touted as the answer to poor school districts with old buildings, with the emphasis on financial returns rather than on student welfare and educational development.

Etch-a-Sketch mentality. A mind-set where educators, in search of quick fixes to their problems, move in one specific direction until "experts" turn the knobs and take them to another direction.

Flow. An organizational element where the efforts of a group of individuals over time will affect the organization.

Focus Group. A small group of individuals brought together to respond to a set of questions. The responses of the group are usually recorded as data and used to inform a line of inquiry.

Inquiry Process. A process in which an individual or a group of individuals systematically examine a problem or question based on evidence and generate conclusions and/or solutions based on that evidence. Often this process requires gathering the evidence or data through a variety of techniques.

Interviews. A data gathering procedure that allows individuals to respond to specific questions. The responses are recorded and used as data to respond to a line of inquiry.

Levers of change. This concept was articulated by Peter Senge in his work, *The Fifth Discipline*. According to Senge, levers are actions that bring about change because they alter the behavior of the organization as well as the individual.

National education goals. National goals established by U.S. governors on September 28, 1989, whereby they decided for the first time to establish *national education goals* that would "guarantee an internationally competitive standard" in six areas by the year 2000.

NCLB. No Child Left Behind is federal legislation that was signed into law in January 2002. According to this law, in order to receive federal aid, every state must put into place a set of academic standards along with a detailed testing plan to determine whether those standards are being met. Students who are in schools that do not meet the standards established by the state may move to other schools in the district, and schools that regularly fail to make annual yearly progress (AYP) will be subject to corrective action. The act uses what it refers to as "annual yearly progress" as one of the main measures of a school's performance. This law requires that schools must demonstrate that their students are making progress each year. It also mandates that schools set equal increments of improvement in order to achieve 100 percent proficiency by the school year 2012–2013. In addition to ensuring that the entire school has reached a level of proficiency by 2012–2013, the school must also show how particular subgroups are also making progress. These subgroups include various races and ethnicities, economically disadvantaged students, students with disabilities, and students with limited English proficiency.

Nonlinearity. An organizational element where unpredictable outcomes from efforts and points to the fact that there is not always a one-to-one correspondence between level of action and degree of result.

Organizational Analysis. A process involves a systematic examination of an organization including such organizations as a school, a school district, a community, or a business. The information acquired through the analysis process is often used to respond to a line of inquiry.

Organizational theory. Using ideas about people, leadership, and organizational structure to understand what happens within organizations.

Parent associations. Groups of parents formed outside of the governance of the school. These groups often organize in order to provide support for the school and to get parents within the community involved in the school.

Parent Center. A governance model for schools that is created and sustained by parents to help parents get involved in the school community.

Professional accountability. It requires teachers to make their own decisions concerning students, and therefore assumes a high level of competency and knowledge.

Qualitative research. Research that gathers descriptive information through individuals' stories, comments, and actions. Qualitative research often uses interviews, focus groups, and observations among other techniques in order to get descriptive information to increase one's understanding of phenomenon or to answer questions that are not limited to quantifiable information.

Quantitative research. Research that gathers numerical data to respond to questions with measurable outcomes. Quantitative research often uses surveys, analysis of test scores, and use of other numerical information (census data, etc.).

Reform canons. The manner in which schools and/or districts adopt reform ideas completely and without question.

Stakeholders. Any individual who has something at stake in a school, community, or whatever the subject of concern may be.

Structural inequalities. Any elements within a school, community, or within society in general that perpetuate unfair or unequal conditions for individuals or groups of individuals.

Study Circles. Groups of typically eight to twelve people who come together for a series of meetings during a limited period of time in order to explore issues or to learn about a specific topic.

Survey. An instrument designed to answer questions about a line of inquiry. The questions are given to an appropriate number of individuals, and the responses are recorded and used as data to respond to a line of inquiry.

Systematic observation. A deliberate way of watching what is going on in one's setting. Often individuals use observation instruments to help guide their observations and to make them more systematic. This helps ensure that observers are looking at the same thing in a number of observations. It also helps ensure that the observer is looking specifically at whatever he or she intended to observe.

Tagging. An organizational element where the use of symbols or rituals to form a common identity among individuals within an organization.

Trajectory of action. A state of being in which schools and districts adopt reform canons and, by virtue of adopting the canons, act in a particular way that excludes other possibilities.

Urban education. Schooling in a central city or otherwise metropolitan area.

Urban school systems. Bureaucratic organizations and have a large number of people running them at a central level. The roles these individuals play within the systems are often technical, controlled, and part of a complex hierarchy of decision makers.

Resources

WEB SITE RESOURCES FOR EDUCATORS

Constructing school partnerships with parents and community, http://www.ncrel.org/sdrs/areas/issues/envrnmnt/famncomm/pa400.htm.

Critical issue: Supporting ways parents and families can become involved in schools, http://www.ncrel.org/sdrs/areas/issues/envrnmnt/famncomm/pa100.htm.

Developing successful partnership programs, http://www.naesp.org/ContentLoad.do?contentId=1121.

Engaging parents in education: Lessons from five parental information and resource centers, http://www.ed.gov/admins/comm/parents/parentinvolve/report_pg7.html.

Examples of schools that involve parents, http://www.ncrel.org/sdrs/areas/issues/envrnmnt/famncomm/pa1lk23.htm.

The Family Involvement Network of Educators, http://www.gse.harvard.edu/hfrp/projects/fine.html.

NAESP spotlight on promising practices: Helping principals create cultures of engagement in their schools, http://www.naesp.org/client_files/SharingDream.pdf.

National Clearinghouse for English Language Acquisition, http://www.ncela.gwu.edu/resabout/parents/4_models.html.

Parental involvement from a practitioner's perspective, http://www.ed.gov/admins/comm/parents/webcast/pntinvwebcast.html.

Parent involvement at the middle school level, http://www.middleweb.com/ParntInvl.html.

Teacher tools: Improving communication, http//sde.state.nm.us/div/rural_ed/toolkit/teacher_tools/improving_communication.html.

Teacher tools: Working with the community module, http://sde.state.nm.us/div/rural_ed/toolkit/teacher_tools/collaborating_community.html.

Toolkits for helping schools and families work together, http://sde.state.nm.us/div/rural_ed/toolkit/index.html.

WEB SITE RESOURCES FOR PARENTS, FAMILIES, AND COMMUNITIES

Anie E. Casey Foundation Knowledge Center, http://www.aecf.org/Knowledge Center/Publications.aspx?pubguid={F34592C1-0498-440C-A527-3C82F23775E6}.

Annenberg Institute for School Reform: Community Involvement, http://www.annenberginstitute.org/cip/.

Assessing school-community collaboration, http://www.ed.gov/admins/lead/safety/training/partnerships/assessingcom.pdf.

Community commitment, http://www.ed.gov/pubs/Compact/appB.html.

Family, school, and community involvement in school-age child care programs: Best practices, http://www.joe.org/joe/1996june/a3.html.

National Coalition for Parent Involvement in Education (NCPIE), http://www.ncpie.org/.

NCLB, facts and terms every parent should know about, http://www.ed.gov/nclb/overview/intro/parents/parentfacts.html.

NCPIE, evidence of impact of school, family, and community involvement on student achievement, http://www.ncpie.org/WhatsHappening/researchJanuary2006.html.

NCPIE, evidence of impact of school, family, and community involvement on student achievement, http://www.ncpie.org/WhatsHappening/researchJanuary2006.html.

NCPIE, resources for administrators, http://www.ncpie.org/Resources/Administrators.cfm.

NCPIE, resources for educators, http://www.ncpie.org/Resources/Educators.cfm.

NCPIE, resources for parents and family, http://www.ncpie.org/Resources/ParentsFamilies.cfm.

Parent and community involvement strategies that work, http://www.educationworld.com/a_admin/admin/admin192.shtml.

Parents as Teachers, http://www.parentsasteachers.org/site/pp.asp?c=ekIRLcMZJxE&b=272091.

Parent engagement as a school reform strategy, http://www.ericdigests.org/1998-3/reform.html.

Parent involvement in education: A resource for parents, administrators, and communities, http://web.archive.org/web/20031202171331/http://npin.org/library/pre1998/n00321/n00321.html.

Parent partnerships boost student achievement, http://cleweb.org/parent.htm.

Parent partnerships facilitated by the Office of Civil Rights, http://www.ed.gov/parents/needs/rights/ocr/parents2.html.

Parents write their worlds: A parent involvement program bridging urban schools and families, http://www.gse.harvard.edu/hfrp/projects/fine/resources/digest/urban.html.

Project Appleseed: A national campaign for public school improvement, http://www.projectappleseed.org/.

Schools, questions parents ask about, http://www.ed.gov/parents/academic/help/questions/index.html.

Summer home learning recipes, http://www.ed.gov/pubs/Recipes/index.html.

Urban Strategies Council, http://www.urbanstrategies.org/index.html.

ADDITIONAL RESOURCES

Aronson, J. Z. (April 1996). How schools can recruit hard-to-reach parents. *Educational Leadership*, 53 (7), 58–60.

Ascher, C. (March 1988). Improving the school-home connection for low-income urban parents. *ERIC Digest*, Available online: http://www.eric.ed.gov/contentdelivery/servlet/ERICServlet?accno=ED293973.

Ballen, J., and Moles, O. (September 1994). *Strong Families, Strong Schools: Building Community Partnerships for Learning*. Washington, DC: U.S. Department of Education. Available online: http://eric-web.tc.columbia.edu/families/strong/

Briggs, X. (1998). *Doing Democracy up Close: Culture, Power, and Community in Community Planning*. Cambridge, MA: Harvard University, Kennedy School of Government.

Center on Families, Communities, Schools, and Children's Learning. (1994). *Parent involvement: The Relationship between School-to-Home Communication and Parents' Perceptions and Beliefs*. Baltimore, MD: Johns Hopkins University.

Chrispeels, J., Boruta, M., and Daugherty, M. (1988). *Communicating with Parents*. San Diego, CA: San Diego County Office of Education.

Cibulka, J. G. and Kritek, W. J., eds. (1996). *Coordination among Schools, Families, and Communities: Prospects for Educational Reform*. Albany, NY: State University of New York Press.

Cochran, M. and Dean, C. (1991). Home-school relations and the empowerment process. *The Elementary School Journal*, 91(3), 261–269.

Cortez, E. (1994). *Engaging the Public: One Way to Organize*. Rochester, MN: National Alliance for Restructuring Education.

Dauber, S. L., and Epstein, J. L. (1993). Parent attitudes and practices of involvement in inner-city elementary and middle schools. In N. F. Chavkin (Ed.), *Families and Schools in a Pluralistic Society*. Albany, NY: State University of New York Press, 455–480.

Davies, D. (1991). Schools reaching out: Family, school and community partnerships for student success. *Phi Delta Kappan*, 72 (5), 376–382.

DeKanter, A., Ginsburg, A. L., Pederson, J., Peterson, T. K., and Rich, D. (1997). *A Compact for Learning: An Action Handbook for Family-School-Community Partnerships*, Available online: http://www.ed.gov/pubs/Compact/.

Eastman, G. (1988). *Family Involvement in Education*. Madison, WI: Wisconsin Department of Public Instruction.

Epstein, J. (1987). Parent involvement: What research says to administrators. *Education and Urban Society*, 19(2), 119–136.

Epstein, J. (1995). School/family/community partnerships: Caring for the children we share. *Phi Delta Kappan*, 76 (9), 701–712.

Epstein, J. and Jansen, N. (2004). Developing successful partnership programs. *Principal—Connecting with Families*. 83(3), 10–15.

Erickson, B. (2003). Social networks: The value of variety. *Contexts*, 2(1), 25–31.

Families and Work Institute. (1994). *Employers, Families, and Education: Facilitating Family Involvement in Learning*. New York: Author.

Fruchter, N. and Gray, R. (2006). Community engagement: Mobilizing constituents to demand and support educational improvement. *Voices in Urban Education*. Providence, RI: The Annenburg Institute for School Reform.

Funkhouser, J. E., and Gonzales, M. R. (1997). *Family Involvement in Children's Education: Successful Local Approaches. An Idea Book.* Available online: http://www.ed.gov/pubs/FamInvolve/.

Gold, E., Simon, E., and Brown, C. (2002). *Successful Community Organizing for School Reform: Strong Neighborhoods, Strong Schools.* Chicago, IL: Cross City Campaign for Urban School Reform and Research for Action.

Henderson, A., and Berla, N., eds. (1994). *A New Generation of Evidence: The Family Is Critical to Student Achievement.* Washington, DC: National Committee for Citizens in Education, Center for Law and Education.

Henderson, A., and Mapp, K. L. (2002). *A New Wave of Evidence: The Impact of School, Family, and Community Connections on Student Achievement.* Austin, TX: Southwest educational development laboratory.

Hickman, C. W. (December 1995 to January 1996). *The Future of High School Success: The Importance of Parent Involvement Programs* Available online: http://horizon.unc.edu/projects/hsj/hickman.asp.

Hill, P. T. (2000). *Getting Serious about Urban School Reform.* Washington, DC: Brookings Institution Press.

Jehl, J. (2007). *Connecting Schools, Families, and Communities: Stories and Results from the Annie E. Casey Foundation's Education Investments.* Baltimore, MD: The Annie E. Casey Foundation.

Jordon, A. (2006). *Tapping the Power of Social Networks: Understanding the Role of Social Networks in Strengthening Families and Transforming Communities.* Baltimore, MD: The Annie E. Casey Foundation.

Kingsbury, K. J. (1991). *A Guide for Parent Involvement.* St. Paul, MN: Minnesota Department of Education.

Kirshner, B., O'Donoghue, J. L., and McLaughlin, M. W., eds. (2002). *Youth Participation: Improving Institutions and Communities.* San Francisco, CA: Jossey-Bass.

Lewis, A. (1992). *Helping Young Urban Parents Educate Themselves and Their Children* [Online]. Available: http://eric-web.tc.columbia.edu/digests/dig85.html.

Liontos, L. (1993, November). *How Can I Be Involved in My Child's Education?* [Online]. Available: http://www.kidsource.com/kidsource/content2/How.Involved.html.

Medriatta, K. (2004). *Constituents of Change: Community Organizations and Public Education Reform.* New York: New York University, Institute for educational and social policy.

Mediratta, K., Shah, S., McAlister, S., Fruchter, N., Mokhtar, C., & Lockwood, D. (2008). *Organized Communities, Stronger Schools: A Preview of Research Findings.* Providence, RI: Annenberg Institute for School Reform at Brown University.

Moles, O. C. (1996, August). *Reaching All Families: Creating Family-Friendly Schools* [Online]. Available: http://www.ed.gov/pubs/ReachFam/index.html

National Association of Elementary School Principals. (2007). *Sharing the Dream: Stories of Principals Actively Engaging Communities.* Alexandria, VA: National Association of Elementary School Principals.

National Association of Partners in Education. (1989). *Handbook for Principals and Teachers: A Collaborative Approach for the Effective Involvement of*

Resources 163

Community and Business Volunteers at the School Site. Alexandria, VA: Author.

National Network of Partnership Schools. (1997). *Partnership Program* [Online]. Available: http://www.csos.jhu.edu/p2000/program.htm

National Parent Teacher Association. (1990). *School Is What We Make It!* [planning kit]. Chicago, IL: Author.

Nathan, J., & Radcliffe, B. (1994). *It's Apparent: We Can and Should Have More*

North Central Regional Educational Laboratory. (1993). Integrating community services for young children and their families. *NCREL Policy Brief*, Report 3. Available online: http://www.ncrel.org/sdrs/areas/issues/envrnmnt/go/93-3toc.htm.

North Central Regional Educational Laboratory. (January 1996). School-community collaboration. *New Leaders for Tomorrow's Schools*, 2(1). Available online: http://www.ncrel.org/cscd/pubs/lead21/2-1toc.htm.

Radcliffe, B., and Nathan, J. (1994). *Training for Parent Partnership: Much More Should Be Done.* Minneapolis, MN: University of Minnesota, Humphrey Institute of Public Affairs, Center for School Change.

Rioux, J. W., and Berla, N. (1993). *Innovations in Parent and Family Involvement.* Princeton Junction, NJ: Eye on Education.

Rutherford, B. (1995). *Creating Family/School Partnerships.* Columbus, OH: National Middle School Association.

Rutherford, B., Anderson, B., and Billig, S. (1995). *Studies of Education Reform: Parent and Community Involvement in Education. Final Technical Report. Vol. 1: Findings and Conclusions.* Available online: http://www.ed.gov/pubs/SER/ParentComm/.

Sanders, M. (1997). *Building Effective School-Family-Community Partnerships in Large Urban Districts.* Washington, DC: Office of Educational Research and Improvement. Available online: http://www.eric.ed.gov/ERICDocs/data/ericdocs2sql/content_storage_01/0000019b/80 /16/a3/c9.pdf.

Schwartz, W. (1994). *A Guide to Creating a Parent Center in an Urban School* Available online: http://eric-web.tc.columbia.edu/guides/pg14.html.

Sebring, P. B., Allensworth, A. S., Bryk, J., Easton, Q., and Luppescu, S. (2006). *The Essential Supports for School Improvement.* Chicago, IL: Consortium on Chicago School Research.

Shartrand, A. M., Weiss, H. B., Kreider, H. M., and Lopez, M. L. (1997). *New Skills for New Schools: Preparing Teachers in Family Involvement* Available online: http://www.ed.gov/pubs/NewSkills/.

Shields, P. M. (September 1994). *Bringing Schools and Communities Together in Preparation for the 21st Century: Implications of the Current Educational Reform Movement for Family and Community Involvement Policies.* Available online: http://www.ed.gov/pubs/EdReformStudies/SysReforms/shields1.html.

Swap, S. (1993). *Developing Home-School Partnerships.* New York: Teacher's College Press.

Swick, K. (1991). *Teacher-Parent Partnerships to Enhance School Success in Early Childhood Education.* Washington, DC: National Education Association.

Swick, K. (1992). *Teacher-Parent Partnerships.* Available online: http://www.ericfacility.net/ericdigests/ed351149.html.

U.S. Department of Education. (1994). *Connecting Families and Schools to Help Our Children Succeed*. Available online: http://www.ed.gov/PressReleases/02-1994/parent.html.

U.S. Department of Education. (1997). *Achieving the Goals. Goal 8: Parent Involvement and Participation*. Available online: http://www.ed.gov/pubs/AchGoal8.

Williams, D., and Stallworth, J. (1984). *Parent Involvement in Education Project*. Austin, TX: Southwest Educational Development Laboratory.

Yates, L. (1993). *Building a Successful Parent Center in an Urban School*. Available Online: http://www.ericfacility.net/databases/ERIC_Digests/ed358198.html.

Index

About the Authors

DONNA ADAIR BREAULT is Associate Professor of Curriculum and Educational Leadership at Georgia State University. Her research focuses on Deweyan inquiry and the role it plays in curriculum, educational research, and the creation and support of public space for action and advocacy. Her scholarship includes the coedited book, *Experiencing Dewey: Insights into the Classroom* as well as articles in *Educational Theory, The Journal of Thought, Educational Forum, Educational Studies,* and *Planning and Changing* among others.

LOUISE ANDERSON ALLEN is Associate Professor of Educational Leadership at South Carolina State University. A former classroom teacher, school and central staff administrator in the public schools of Charleston, South Carolina, Allen was awarded the first postdoctoral fellowship given by the Avery African-American Research Center at the College of Charleston. Her most recent publications appear in the *Journal of Curriculum and Pedagogy, Journal of Personnel Evaluation in Education, Journal of Cases in Educational Leadership, Journal of the Gilded Age and Progressive Era,* and the *International Journal of Urban Educational Leadership.* She is also the author of *A Bluestocking in Charleston: The Life and Career of Laura Bragg* and is a coauthor of the second edition of *Turning Points in Curriculum: A Contemporary American Memoir.*